In this manga, the term *osore* (fear or awe) is used. I think this relates to how we feel when we think that someone is "cool" or "cute."

I'd like to keep creating characters who make us feel this way.

—HIROSHI SHIIBASHI, 2008

HIROSHI SHIIBASHI debuted in BUSINESS JUMP magazine with *Aratama*. NURA: RISE OF THE YOKAI CLAN is his breakout hit. He was an assistant to manga artist Hirohiko Araki, the creator of *Jojo's Bizarre Adventure*. *Steel Ball Run* by Araki is one of his favorite manga.

NURA: RISE OF THE YOKAI CLAN

NURA: RISE OF THE YOKAI CLAN
VOLUME 1
SHONEN JUMP Manga Edition

Story and Art by HIROSHI SHIIBASHI

Translation – AltJapan Ltd., Yumi Okamoto,
Cindy Yamauchi
Adaptation – AltJapan Ltd., Mark Giambruno
Touch-up Art and Lettering – Gia Cam Luc, Rina Mapa
Graphics and Cover Design – Fawn Lau
Editor – Daniel Gillespie

Printed in the U.S.A.

Published by VIZ Media, LLC
P.O. Box 77010
San Francisco, CA 94107

10 9 8 7 6 5 4 3 2 1
First printing, February 2011

www.viz.com www.shonenjump.com

NURA: RISE OF THE YOKAI CLAN

1

BECOMING THE LORD OF PANDEMONIUM

STORY AND ART BY
HIROSHI SHIIBASHI

TABLE OF CONTENTS

NURA: RISE OF THE YOKAI CLAN

1

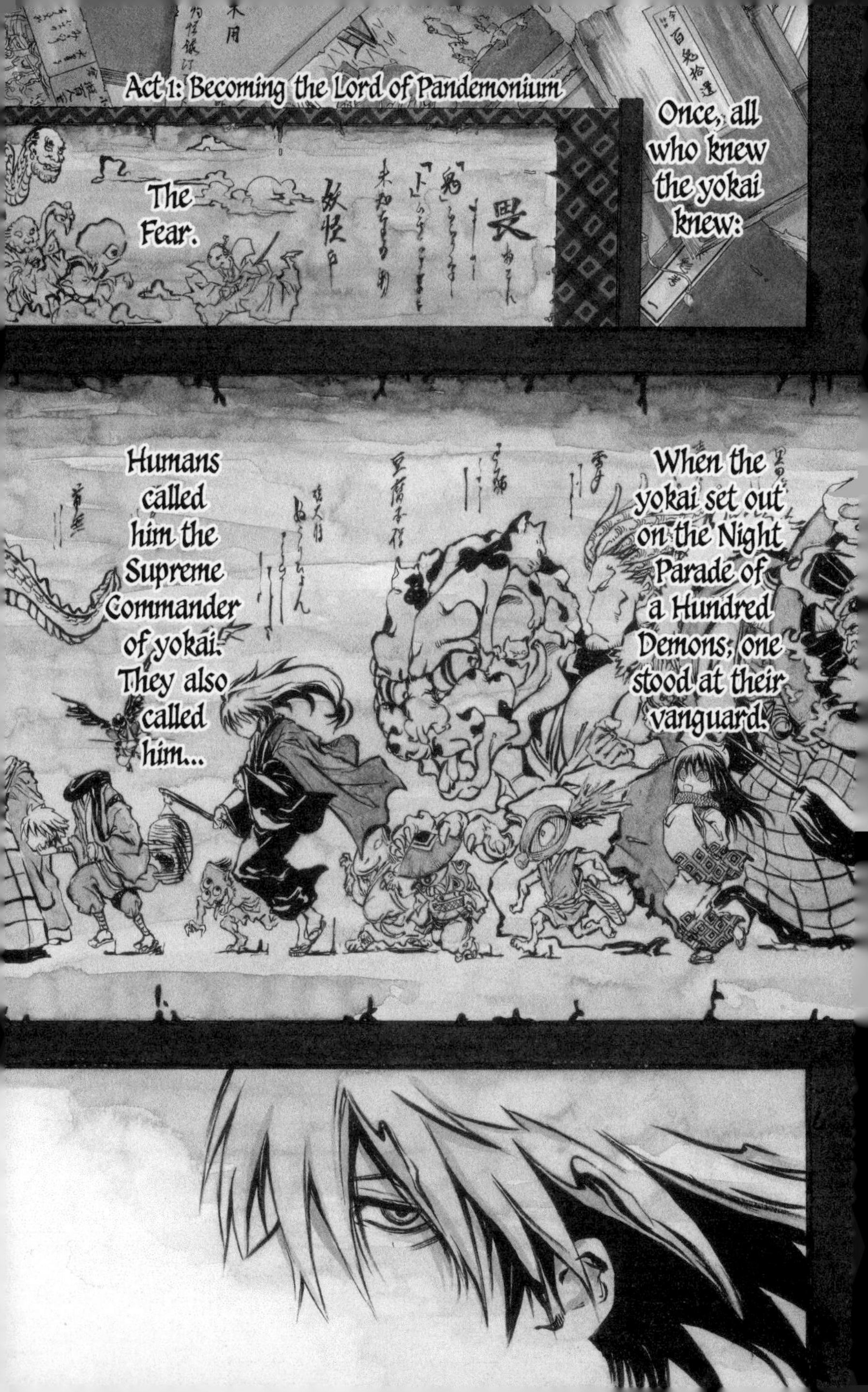
Act 1: Becoming the Lord of Pandemonium
Once, all who knew the yokai knew:
The Fear.
When the yokai set out on the Night Parade of a Hundred Demons, one stood at their vanguard.
Humans called him the Supreme Commander of yokai. They also called him...

Nurarihyon,
the Lord of Pandemonium.
Act 1: Becoming the Lord of Pandemonium

ぬらりひょんのクォーターで奴良リクオ
Rikuo Nura, One-Quarter Nurarihyon

In a village on the Kanto Plain...
...called Ukiyoe Town...
There is said to be...
...a yokai clan feared by locals, even today.
SWIP
SWIP
MASTER?
MASTER?!
OOH... NGH...
TPTPTP
OH!
IS SOMETHING THE MATTER?
...
UGH OOF
LORD RIKUO?!
ARE YOU FEELING SICK?
TP TP
TP TP TP
NGH GUH

YOINK
EH?!
SHA
SPROOOING
WAH?!
FWOOP
???
??
HA HA HA
GOTCHA!! I CAUGHT A YOKAI!
EH? EH?
EHHH?
FWOOM
AH, YUKI-ONNA!
EASY PICKINGS, LIKE ALWAYS!
Rikuo Nura
Age 8 (Third Grade)
TEE HEE
HEY!!
WHAT THE...?! MASTER!!
AH HA HA
SCOPE
SCOPE
HOW FAR DID SHE GO SEARCHING FOR...
AH!

WSH
YUKI-ONNA?! WHAT THE DEVIL ARE YOU DOING?!
WHO DID THIS TO YOU?!
LET ME DOWN...
KRASH
HUH?!
KRCH
KRCH
WHAT-GRAHH-HHH!
KRCH
KRCH
I'M FALLING! I'M FALLING!
KRCH
H-HE GOT US AGAIN!
HA HA!
AH!!
HEY, YOU GUYS!
M-MASTER, WAIT...
YOUNG MASTER! I KNEW IT!
YOU'RE JUST LIKE THE SUPREME COM-MANDER...
...YOU ALWAYS TAKE IT TOO FAR!!
DOOOM

GOMP
GOMP
GOMP
AND THEN... AND THEN... GET THIS, GRAMPS!
THEY WERE ALL SCARED! EVEN THOUGH THEY'RE YOKAI.
DOOM
HEY! HEY! SO, CAN I HAVE IT?
THE TITLE OF *THE THIRD*?!
HA HA HA!
WELL DONE.
BUT YOKAI SHOULD NEVER LET ANYONE GET THE DROP ON THEM.
Yokai Supreme Commander **Nurarihyon**
HM?
YOU'LL HAVE TO WAIT A LITTLE LONGER... UNTIL YOU'RE A LITTLE BIT OLDER AND BECOME YOKAI-LIKE.
REALLY?!
I'M GONNA TRY MY BEST!
I'M GONNA TRY MY BEST TO BE A GREAT YOKAI SUPREME COMMANDER LIKE YOU, GRAMPS!

HAHA. I LOOK FORWARD TO THAT.
PFF
GRAMPS, ARE YOKAI REALLY SO GREAT? AND STRONG?
THEY SURE DON'T SEEM LIKE IT...
BITE YOUR TONGUE, RIKUO!
DOM
HAVE YOU FORGOTTEN MY STORY?!
SNORT
TELL IT AGAIN! TELL IT AGAIN!
I LOVE THAT STORY!
YOKAI...
...CAN HARNESS THE POWER OF THE SUPER-NATURAL TO FLY THROUGH THE SKY, AND HAVE PHYSICAL ABILITIES AND FORMS BEYOND THE IMAGINATIONS OF MORTALS!
BACK IN MY PRIME, I COMMANDED A YOKAI ARMY A HUNDRED STRONG THAT TERRORIZED HUMANS NIGHT AFTER NIGHT...
THEY FEARED US.
AND AS THE YOKAI SUPREME COMMANDER, DO YOU KNOW WHAT HUMANS CALLED ME?
THE LORD OF THE NIGHT!
COOOOOL!
YOU'RE SO COOL, GRAMPS!
THE YOKAI PLEDGED THEIR LOYALTY TO ME. THEY WORK FOR ME TO THIS VERY DAY.
THEY TAKE CARE OF YOU AND ME BOTH, SO WATCH YOUR TONGUE.
OKAY!
NOW, RIKUO...
I'LL SHOW YOU SOME YOKAI MAGIC!
HUH?
WHERE'D THAT CUSTOMER GO?

KIDS, DON'T TRY THIS AT HOME...OR ANYWHERE!
AHH!! THEY PULLED A DINE AND DASH!!
HA HA HA HA HA
WHADDYA THINK? PRETTY GREAT, HUH?
THAT "SPELL" LETS YA EAT FOR FREE!
TO!
TO!
IT'S AWESOME, GRANPA!
TO!
FWO--M
LORD RIKUO!
GOOD MORNING!
YOU'RE LOOKING CHIPPER TODAY!
LORD RIKUO, YOU NEED TO GET DRESSED.
YOU'LL BE LATE FOR SCHOOL!
Kubinashi
Yuki-Onna
HEY! YOU TWO!
Karasu-Tengu
FLAP FLAP
STOP SLACKING OFF! HELP THE MASTER GET READY!
OKAY!
HERE YOU GO, MASTER! WE WASHED YOUR HAIR, NOW LET'S DRY IT OFF--
GAHAHAHA
Aotabo
Kurotabo
HEH HEH HEH HEH
RUB RUB RUB RUB
OW OW OW!
MASTER! YOUR SHOES!
BANG
AND SOCKS!
BONG
AND YOUR FOOT-BATH!
BING
YOU'VE GOT IT BACK-WARDS!!
MAN... GET IT TOGETHER, GUYS!

RIKUO, YOU'RE LATE.
THE BUS IS ALREADY HERE.
PITTER PATTER
I TOLD YOU, YOU'RE GONNA MAKE US LATE!
BUT...
KANA!
BRRRM
...EVERY-ONE WAS...
EVERY-ONE WHO?
BRRRM MM
WOW! WHAT A BIG HOUSE!
IS THAT NURA'S PLACE? NO WAY!
WE DID IT. HE'S SAFELY OFF TO SCHOOL.
I SWEAR, HE'S A CHIP OFF THE SUPREME COMMANDER'S BLOCK. WHAT A HANDFUL...
WHEW
HA. JUST WAIT UNTIL HE TAKES OVER!
YEAH, HE IS IN LINE TO BECOME THE THIRD, AFTER ALL.
REALLY? I KNOW HE'S THE SUPREME COMMANDER'S GRANDSON, BUT...
...CAN A *HUMAN* CHILD REALLY RUN THE ENTIRE NURA SYNDICATE?

WAA WAA
DSH
WAA WAA
SIX POINT NINE!!
HFF HFF
CRAP, I LOST!
NURA WON AGAIN!
NURA! HOW COME YOU'RE SO FAST NOW?!
I MEAN, YOU CAN REALLY BLAZE!
YAMMER YAMMER
WHAT MAKES YOU BETTER THAN ME?
HAHA... IT'S BECAUSE OF GRAMPS.
HE'S THE SUPREME COMMANDER OF YOKAI!
?
YOKAI?!
IS THAT... GOOD?
IT'S GREAT! GRAMPS TOLD ME SO!
WOW.

Presentation Day
YAMMER
CHATTER
CHATTER
YAMMER
...AND SO, THE FEARSOME, CHILD-DEVOURING YOKAI WERE DRIVEN AWAY BY THE HANDSOME ONMYOJI...
LOCAL RESEARCH GROUP 1
...AND THE SHRINE BUILT IN HIS HONOR IS WHAT'S KNOWN TODAY AS THE ARATAMA SHRINE!
THE END.
THAT CONCLUDES OUR GROUP'S REPORT ON LOCAL MYTHOLOGY.
WHOA
CLAP CLAP
GAH!
SO, THEY USED TO BE HERE!
YOKAI STORIES ARE SO SCARY!
YAMM
YIKES!
EEK
EEK
SENSEI, HOW MANY POINTS DID WE GET?
ONE HUNDRED!
THAT'S OUR KIYOTSUGU!
EH?!
H-HOLD ON, WHAT WAS SO GREAT ABOUT THAT SPEECH?!
YOKAI...
...ARE GOOD GUYS!

SILENCE...
EH?
W-WHA?
I MEAN, THEY DO SCREW UP A LOT...
...BUT AOTABO'S REALLY STRONG, AND YUKI-ONNA'S GREAT AT COOLING OFF FOOD.
YAMMER
HUH? WHAT'S THAT KID TALKING ABOUT?
HEY, YOU!!
ARE YOU TALKING TRASH ABOUT KIYOTSUGU'S REPORT?!
HUH?!
HE ALWAYS WAS KINDA WEIRD...
IT'S TRUE!!
I KNOW, 'CAUSE MY GRAMPS IS THE YOKAI SUPREME COMMANDER!!
RIKUO?
REALLY, NOW.
MURMUR
I SUPPOSE THAT MAKES YOUR GRANDFATHER "NURARIHYON"?
HMPH
MURMUR
?!
YEAH!!
HOW'DJA KNOW?!
IS HE FAMOUS?
YOU FOOL. "NURARIHYON"...
...IS A YOKAI THAT SNEAKS INTO PEOPLE'S HOMES, EATS THEIR FOOD AND PLAYS SILLY TRICKS ON THEM. HE'S THE MOST PETTY YOKAI EVER.
WHAT'S SO GREAT ABOUT THAT?
EH? THAT'S SO UNCOOL.
DISGUST-ING!

HA HA... BUT, DON'T SWEAT IT. YOKAI ARE JUST FAIRY TALES CREATED BY PEOPLE A LONG TIME AGO!
HUSH
...
THEY DON'T REALLY EXIST!
I'D, LIKE, DIE IF I REALLY SAW ONE!
YEAH!
JUST... JUST HOLD ON A MINUTE!!
MY HOUSE... MY HOUSE... IS FULL OF—
THAT'S RIGHT! YOU TELL HIM, KIYOTSUGU!
YOU ARE REALLY CREEPING EVERYONE OUT, NURA!
YOU'RE SUCH A BRAT!! AND KIYOTSUGU IS SO GROWN-UP!
YOKAI... DON'T... EXIST!
SHOCK!!
WHAT'S THE MATTER, LORD RIKUO?
YOU SEEM DOWN.
YEAH.
A LITTLE.
WELL, CHEER UP. THERE'S A MEETING OF CLAN LEADERS TODAY.
THE SUPREME COMMANDER WILL CALL ON YOU.
TP
GRAMPS WILL?
TP

TOMP
TOMP
TOMP
TODAY'S THE BIG MEETING OF THE CLAN...
YOKAI FROM ALL OVER THE COUNTRY. I'VE NEVER SEEN THIS MANY TOGETHER!
WOW!
AMAZING!
TOMP
TOMP
TOMP
MURMUR

YAMMER
YAMMER
FWSH
FWSH
MURMUR
C'MON, ONE DRINK.
SORRY, I GAVE IT UP.
MURMUR
MURMUR
I'M AT MY WIT'S END. HUMANS SIMPLY DON'T FEAR YOKAI ANYMORE.
WE'RE OLD-FASHIONED.
HA HA HA
THAT FIRE IN ARATAMA VILLAGE? MINE.
WELL, I HEARD YOU PULLED ONE OFF YOURSELF THE OTHER DAY...
WHAT? YOU HAVEN'T HEARD?
YOU KNOW...
IF YOU'RE TALKING EVILDOING, YOU'VE GOT TO MENTION LORD GAGOZE.
OOH, IT'S THE SUPREME COMMANDER!
YAMMER
I THANK ALL OF YOU FOR COMING.
HOW IS EVERYONE?
SCARING THE WORLD AS USUAL, I HOPE?
HEHEHE. TRICKS AIN'T WHAT THEY USED TO BE.
WHAT BROUGHT ON THIS MEETING, SUPREME COMMANDER?
RIGHT...
THE TIME HAS COME TO NAME THE THIRD.
SNIK

WELL DONE, SUPREME COMMANDER.
IT'S BEEN SEVERAL YEARS SINCE THE SECOND PASSED AWAY. IT MUST WEIGH ON YOU, AS THE FIRST, TO COME OUT OF RETIREMENT IN HIS STEAD.
Ha ha ha...
Nura Clan Chairman
Gagoze
The soul of an evil man who attacks the children of priests in the temple at which he was buried. A vicious, child-devouring yokai.
SUPREME COMMANDER! WHEN IT COMES TO EVILDOING, THERE'S NONE BETTER THAN LORD GAGOZE!
FLATTER FLATTER
ALL OF THE MISSING CHILDREN THIS YEAR WERE PERSONALLY HANDLED BY HIS GROUP!
NO, NO. SENDING CHILDREN TO THE DEPTHS IS MERELY MY DUTY!
PLEASE! YOU'RE A PARAGON OF YOKAI VIRTUE!
HA HA HA
WA HA HA HA
HMPH.
I SEE.
YOU'RE A HARD WORKER, GAGOZE!
AT YOUR SERVICE, SUPREME COM-MANDER.

BUT... YOU AREN'T RIGHT FOR THIS JOB.
FOR THE ROLE OF THIRD... I PROPOSE MY GRANDSON, RIKUO!
?!
W-WHAT?!
YAMMER
LORD RIKUO?! REALLY?
YAMMER
YAMMER
HE'S BUT A CHILD!
HE HAS YOUR BLOOD, BUT STILL...
WHAT'S WRONG, GAGOZE? YOU DON'T LOOK SO GOOD.
I-I'M PERFECTLY FINE, MOKUGYO!
...
GRAMPS ...?
YAMMER
WHAT'S THE MATTER, RIKUO?
I THOUGHT THIS WAS WHAT YOU WANTED.
YAMMER

EH?
YOU CAN'T ESCAPE YOUR BLOODLINE.
YOU TAKE AFTER ME, AND THEY ALL KNOW IT.
LET'S HAVE A VOTE!
I CHOOSE YOU TO BE HEIR TO THE CLAN, RIKUO!
THE 72 CLANS OF THE NURA SYNDICATE, SOME TEN THOUSAND YOKAI STRONG, WILL BE YOURS TO COMMAND!
NUH... NO!!
WHAT?
I... I'M NOT LIKE THEM!
EVERYONE... WOULD JUST HATE ME EVEN MORE!
RIKUO ...?
I DIDN'T KNOW THE YOKAI WERE EVIL!
I'M NOTHING LIKE YOU, GRAMPS!
GAH!
NOTHING AT ALL!
DSH

RIKUO, YOU UN-GRATEFUL BRAT!
RIKUO ...
MUTTER
... SUPREME COM-MANDER ...
MUTTER
PARDON MY INSOLENCE... BUT IS HE REALLY OF YOUR BLOODLINE?
Nura Syndicate General Counsel Mokugyo-Daruma
HIS BODY, FORM AND SOUL ALL APPEAR HUMAN TO ME...
HEH HEH HEH... MOST TROUBLING.
SO?!
IT APPEARS THE YOUNG MASTER ...
...HAS SOME GROWING UP TO DO.
...
SUPREME COMMANDER... TIMES ARE HARSH, FOR ALL OF US.
WHY DON'T WE RECITE THE VOW WE PLEDGED TO THE NURA CLAN CREST?

WE YOKAI MUST BE STRONG.
WE MUST MAKE HUMANS KNOW THE FEAR.
MASTER!!
YOU'LL CATCH COLD!
LEAVE ME ALONE!!
...
MASTER ...
THIS IS THE UKIYOE ELEMENTARY STOP.
UKIYOE ELEMENTARY.
BRRM
五井銀行
WHAT'S WRONG, CAN'T YOKAI KIDS TAKE THE BUS?
STOP IT! I DON'T WANT HIM RIDING OUR BUS!
IF HE DOES, WE'LL GET ALL SCARED!
PLUS, HIS HOUSE IS ALL OLD AND RUN-DOWN AND NASTY...
THAT HAUNTED HOUSE? FOR SURE!
AH HA HA HA HA HA!

MAN !!
QUIT MOPING!
THUP
OW!
THE NEXT BUS ISN'T FOR THIRTY MINUTES!
WE GOTTA CATCH THIS ONE! COME ON!
NO...
NOBODY WANTS TO RIDE WITH ME, ANYWAY.
WHY ??
BECAUSE YOU'RE A LIAR?
WRONG !!
I DIDN'T LIE!
I'M ASHAMED OF MYSELF!!
WHAT DO YOU MEAN ?
IT'S BECAUSE I THOUGHT YOKAI WERE COOL...
BUT... ALL THEY DO IS PLAN BAD STUFF.
THEY AREN'T HEROES. THEY'RE *LOSERS*.
KAW KAW
AND...
...I JUST FOLLOWED ALONG, IMITATING GRAMPS.
I DON'T REALLY GET IT, BUT...
...RIKUO...
WHY DON'T YOU JUST DECIDE TO BECOME SOME-ONE WHO *ISN'T* A LOSER?

...
HUH?
REMEMBER WHAT YOU TOLD ME ON THE BUS? ABOUT HOW YOUR YOKAI UNDERLINGS WERE ALWAYS MAKING YOU LATE?
WITH THAT AMAZING HOUSE OF YOURS...IT'S NOT HARD TO BELIEVE SOMETHING WEIRD'S GOING ON IN THERE!
AND IF THERE IS, THEN WHY DON'T YOU USE THAT TO MAKE YOURSELF AN UPSTANDING CITIZEN?
AN UP-STANDING CITIZEN?
FWP
RIGHT! BUT... IF YOU ASK ME...
...YOU SHOULD DROP THAT "YOKAI UNDER-LINGS" TALK.
THAT MEANS ...
...YOU DON'T BELIEVE ME!
WELL, IT SCARES ME!!
YOKAI ARE MONSTERS, RIGHT?
IT SCARES YOU?
IF YOU SHOWED ME, I'D BELIEVE IT...
BUT I DON'T WANNA SEE THEM!!
SIGH...
EVERYONE HATES YOKAI.
I'LL NEVER MENTION THEM AGAIN.

BRRM
CHATTER
TEE HEE
...
IT WAS WORTH A TRY...
BUT RIKUO JUST DOESN'T WANT TO GO HOME.
WHO? NURA?
HEY, NEVER MIND ABOUT NURA. KNOW WHAT I HEARD? THE LEGEND IS *REAL*–
HUH? WHAT LEGEND?
BRRM
THE YOKAI ONE!
KIDS HAVE BEEN DISAPPEAR-ING!
RIGHT AROUND HERE...
S-STOP IT!
OI!! YOU TWO!!
STOP RIGHT THERE!!
TOK TOK TOK TOK TOK TOK TOK TOK TOK
YOKAI DON'T EXIST!! MY RESEARCH PROVED THAT...

GRAAH!

KLOK
KLOK
KAW
KAW
NO MISTAKE.
THAT WAS THE YOUNG MASTER'S BUS.
KAW
KAW

FOR GOODNESS SAKE, LORD RIKUO...
YOU WERE SO LATE THAT I HAD TO COME FIND YOU.
FLAP
FLAP
I CAN'T BELIEVE YOU THOUGHT YOU COULD WALK ALL THAT WAY...
FROM NOW ON, I'M GOING TO MAKE SURE YOU HAVE AN ESCORT, WHETHER YOU LIKE IT OR NOT!
...
KAW
KAW
KARASU-TENGU...
AM I HUMAN OR NOT?
WHAT?
WELL, NOW...
YOUR MOTHER AND GRANDMOTHER WERE HUMAN...
...BUT YOU HAVE THE SUPREME COMMANDER'S BLOOD AS WELL...
I KNOW!
WHICH MEANS THAT YOU'RE ONE-QUARTER YOKAI.
ONE-QUARTER YOKAI?
EXACTLY.
YOU SHOULD FEEL PROUD!
...

READ THIS WAY
LOOK!
TH-THEY'RE BACK!
YAMMER
YAMMER
MASTER!! ARE YOU OKAY?
?
WHAT'S ALL THE FUSS?
BUT...WE THOUGHT...
WAAH
NEWSFLASH! A ROCKSLIDE NEAR THE TUNNEL IN UKIYOE HAS BURIED A BUS!
THE BUS IS BELIEVED TO BE FILLED WITH STUDENTS FROM UKIYOE ELEMENTARY SCHOOL!
?!
WHAT? MY BUS?!
OH, RIKUO, YOU'RE BACK...
YOUR LUCK IS STRONG, AS ALWAYS.

MURMUR
MURMUR
LORD RIKUO IS HOME!
SO, THE RUMORS OF HIS DEMISE WERE UNTRUE!
IT'S TRUE!
I'M SO GLAD...
THE NEXT BUS ISN'T FOR THIRTY MINUTES!
WE GOTTA CATCH THIS ONE! COME ON!
B-BMP
B-BMP
WAAAAAH!! LORD RIKUO!! I WAS SO WORRIED!
BAWL
I WAS EVEN MORE WORRIED, AO!!
CHATTER
ARE YOU SURE YOU'RE OKAY?
OI! BRING SOME HOT WATER!
WE WERE IN SHOCK!
YANK
I'VE GOT TO HELP THEM...
WHERE ARE YOU GOING AT THIS HOUR?!
DSH
SOMEONE GET MY CLOTHES!
ISN'T IT OBVIOUS?

I HAVE TO GO SAVE KANA!
COME ON!! AOTABO!! KURO-TABO!!
EVERY-ONE!
Y-YES, SIR!
WAIT!
STAY WHERE YOU ARE!!
MOKUGYO-DARUMA...?
IT IS FORBID-DEN...
FOR YOKAI TO AID HUMANS IS...AN ABOMINA-TION!!
EH...?
W-WHY?
DO YOU REALLY THINK WE YOKAI CAN FOLLOW AN ORDER LIKE THAT?!
THE NURA SYNDICATE RULES THE YOKAI WORLD!
WE CANNOT UNLEASH PANDEMONIUM AT THE WHIM OF A HUMAN!

LORD DARUMA!! IT'S THE MASTER'S ORDERS!!
IT'S DISRESPECTFUL TO IGNORE THEM!!
DISRESPECTFUL?
HMPH... HAVE YOU FORGOTTEN THAT THE MANDATE OF THE NURA CLAN IS TO BRING *THE FEAR?*
YOKAI EXIST TO INSTILL THE FEAR IN HUMANS.
AND NOW YOU WANT TO HELP THEM? *RIDICULOUS!*
YOU JERK!!
AOTABO?!
UWAH!! IT'S A FIGHT!!
BUT IT'S LORD DARUMA AND AOTABO! WHAT SHOULD WE DO?!
THAT'S...
...ENOUGH!!

THERE'S NO TIME FOR THIS.
SHM
I'VE GOT NO TIME FOR YOUR FOOLISH LOGIC...
...MOKUGYO-DARUMA.
SHM
?
SHM
SHM
LISTEN...
ALL OF YOU...
SHM
MASTER?
THE MASTER IS CHANGING?!
O-OI...
HUH?
?!
IF...
...YOU WON'T LISTEN BECAUSE I'M A HUMAN...
...WILL YOU LISTEN...
SHM
...TO A YOKAI?!
SHF
SHF
SHM

YES? THEN I CAST OFF MY HUMAN-ITY!
EH ?!
WHAT?!
THOSE EYES...
THEY'RE LIKE ANOTHER CREATURE'S!!
ALL OF YOU. FOLLOW ME.
MASTER ?! WAIT!!
LORD MOKUGYO-DARUMA...
I'M BUSY!! TELL ME LATER.

THE FACT THAT LORD RIKUO'S BUS WAS INVOLVED...
...MEANS HE WAS TARGETED ...
...BY AN ASSASSIN... OR...
MASTER!
WE OF THE NURA CLAN MAIN FAMILY WILL FOLLOW YOU!
GAHAHAHA
HEY! I WAS GOING TO SAY THAT FIRST!!
SIP SIP
YAMMER
YAMMER
TONIGHT...
...MY BLOOD... BOILS.
I TOLD YOU, LORD RIKUO.
THAT'S YOUR YOKAI BLOOD.
MY BLOOD ...?
YOUR GRAND-FATHER'S.
B-BMP
MASTER RIKUO... WE ARE YOURS TO COMMAND, BECAUSE...
...YOU HAVE...
TOMP
TOMP
B-BMP

...THE SUPREME COMMANDER'S BLOOD COURSING THROUGH YOUR VEINS!!
ONE-QUARTER IS ENOUGH TO INHERIT HIS LEGACY!!

CLANK
CLANK
NO!!
TAKA-HIRO!!
CLANK
CLANK
SOME-THING ISN'T RIGHT!!
WHAT MADE A ROCKSLIDE HAPPEN HERE?!
THIS ISN'T HAPPENING!
PLEASE! STAY BACK!
THE ROCKS COULD GIVE WAY AGAIN AT ANY TIME!
HELP MY SON, PLEASE!
WHERE'S THE RESCUE SQUAD?!
MAMA...
WHAT'S THAT?
KLATTA KLATTA
OI!! NEED MORE HELP!
MURMUR
MURMUR
WE CAN BREAK THROUGH OVER HERE.

KVIK
NNGH
OOF
IT HURTS—
MOMMY!
IS EVERYONE OKAY?
HANG IN THERE.
WAH!
IENAGA?!
YOU SCARED ME THERE.
B... BUT...
OVER THERE...
I SEE... PEOPLE ...
PEOPLE?
D-DON'T THEY LOOK... KIND OF *WEIRD* TO YOU?
KIYOTSUGU... WHAT ARE THEY?
EH? I-I DON'T KNOW...
TCH...
SOME OF 'EM SURVIVED.

YEEK!!
WH-WHO ARE YOU?!
SHOOO
THE TUNNEL DIDN'T COLLAPSE COMPLETELY...
WE'LL JUST HAVE TO... FINISH THEM OURSELVES.
AND...
YOUNG MASTER AS WELL...
GAHAHA...
EEK!
WAH!
THEY'RE COMING!
SHHP
!!
SHHP
Y...
YOKAI!!

BOOOOM
AA AAA AA AH!
AAA-AAH!
YEEE!!
AHH... AHH ...
AAAAH!

?!
?!
OHO! WE FOUND 'EM, MASTER!
LOOKS LIKE THEY'RE ALIVE!

RRRMMBB
GAGOZE...
YOU RAT... WHY ARE YOU HERE?
L...
LORD GAGOZE...
...
BLASTED MAIN FAMILY...
W-WHAT NOW?!
N-NO WAY... IT CAN'T BE...
KLOMP
THOK
WHAT IS THIS, KIYOTSUGU?!
I...
I DON'T KNOW!
THIS...
...MUST BE SOME KIND OF MISTAKE!

TMP
THERE, THERE... IT'S ALL RIGHT NOW.
CUT IT OUT.
THAT MUG OF YOURS IS ONLY MAKING THINGS WORSE.
YEEK!
Y-YES, MASTER ...
...
I'M SO GLAD YOU'RE OKAY.
KANA...
THIS IS GOING TO BE SCARY, SO CLOSE YOUR EYES.
SWIP
...?
WHO *IS* THAT?

WELL, WELL, IF IT ISN'T MOKUGYO-DARUMA...
DON'T PLAY DUMB WITH ME!
YOU MORON... DO YOU HAVE ANY IDEA WHAT YOU'VE DONE?!
...
LET'S SEE ...
I ATTACKED A BUS-LOAD OF ORDINARY HUMAN BRATS...
WAS THAT WRONG?
!
ARE YOU... SUGGESTING THERE'S A PROBLEM?
GA... GAGOZE ...!!
SO, KILLING KIDS MAKES YOU THINK YOU'RE A BIG SHOT?
?!
IF YOU TRIED TO KILL ME...
...TO TAKE THE TITLE OF *THE THIRD* FOR YOURSELF...
...THEN, GAGOZE ...
...YOU'RE ONE PETTY LITTLE YOKAI.
YOU SNAKE!!
?!
WAIT! THAT'S-
TUP

!
DON'T LAY A FINGER ON LORD RIKUO...
THAT GOES FOR ALL OF YOU GAGOZE CLAN VULTURES...
WHY, YOU...
GAH
!
WHAT ?!
THIS STRING'S MADE FROM JOROGUMO THE SPIDER WOMAN'S WEB AND KEJORO THE COURTESAN'S HAIR. IT'S SPECIAL.
STRUGGLING ONLY MAKES IT TIGHTER.
DON'T MAKE ME LAUGH!
AAA-AH!!

WHAT?!
HE'S...
HE'S... RIKUO?!
SO, HE SURVIVED...
UNFORGIVE-ABLE...
CURSED WRETCH!! KILL HIM!!
KILL THE YOUNG MASTER! RIGHT AWAY!!
AND KILL THOSE LAZY CLOWNS FROM THE MAIN FAMILY TOO!!
ANNIHI-LATE THEM!!
MASTER!!
THWOK
MY TURN!

B—M
GUESS IT'S ALL UP TO STRIKE TEAM LEADER AOTABO.
HEY, I'M A STRIKE TEAM LEADER TOO!!
HUH?
HYUUUUU
IT... IT CAN'T BE...
WE'VE KILLED MORE THAN ANYONE!
WE'RE THE STRONGEST CLAN!

GLARE
GAGOZE, YOU WANT TO BECOME THE LEADER OF THE YOKAI, BUT...
...DO YOU REALLY THINK KILLING ALL THESE HUMANS IS SOMETHING TO BRAG ABOUT?
GIVE IT UP.
GASP
UH...
SHUDDER
IT'S GONNA TAKE MORE THAN CUTTING OFF A FINGER TO MAKE UP FOR THIS LITTLE STUNT.
BLAST...!
HM?
GULP
?!
WHAT THE--?
FWAHAHA-HAHAHA!
WATCH THIS!!
I'LL KILL THEM!!
I'LL KILL THE MASTER'S FRIENDS, UNLESS YOU...
WAAAH!

FWISH
ARRRRGH!
MASTER ?!
OW!
WHY?! WHY A BRAT LIKE YOU?
OW! OW!
WHY... WHY AM I NOT GOOD ENOUGH ?!
I AM...
...THE MOST FEARED YOKAI OF ALL!!
A YOKAI THAT CRAVES AND EATS CHILDREN ...
NATURALLY, YOU'RE FRIGHTENING...
FWISH

BUT A YOKAI WHO TAKES PLEASURE...
...IN KILLING THE WEAK...
...COULD NEVER BE THE LEADER...
...OF THIS DARK WORLD OF OURS.
!!
PATHETIC...
SHFF
IS THIS THE ONLY KIND OF YOKAI IN THE CLAN?
IF THAT'S THE CASE, THEN...
SHFF
...I WILL CERTAINLY BECOME THE THIRD SUPREME COM-MANDER!!
AND ANY YOKAI WHO HAS A PROBLEM WITH HUMANS...
...WILL HAVE A PROB-LEM WITH ME.
MASTER...
AAA-AHH! NOOO!
TELL EVERY YOKAI IN THE WORLD...
...THAT I WILL BE THE LORD OF PANDE-MONIUM!

AND EVERY LAST YOKAI...
...WILL FOLLOW ME IN THE NIGHT PARADE OF A HUNDRED DEMONS!

GRAH...
畏
"THE FEAR."
THE KANJI ITSELF INSPIRES FEAR...
...COMPOSED, AS IT IS, OF THE MEANINGS "DEMON" AND "WHIP."
IT EVOKES EMOTIONS.
A SENSE OF THE UNKNOWN —
—AND OF THE "YOKAI" THEMSELVES.
EVILDOING LIKE GAGOZE'S EVOKES "THE FEAR."
GIANT THINGS EVOKE "THE FEAR". THREATS EVOKE "THE FEAR." AUTHORITY EVOKES "THE FEAR."
HOWEVER— "THE FEAR" IS BUT ONE ASPECT OF YOKAI.

WOW.
HE'S SMALL, BUT...
...SO COOL.
YOKAI... REALLY DO EXIST...
...THEY'RE AMAZING...
I, THE DARUMA... KNEW THIS...
...BUT ONLY TRULY REALIZED IT NOW.
ONE WHO CAN EVOKE AWE, EVEN AMONG HUMANS.
ONE WHO CAN BE REVERED.
FWUMP
...?
LORD RIKUO?

YAMMER
WHAT'S WRONG ?!
?!
HE COL-LAPSED!
YAMMER
IS HE INJURED ?
FSSS
MASTER!
FSSSSS
YAMMER
YAMMER
YAMMER
...
HE'S RETURNING...
...TO HUMAN FORM ...?
?!
CAN IT BE...
...THAT BECAUSE HE'S ONLY ONE-QUARTER YOKAI...
B-BMP
...HE CAN ONLY REMAIN A YOKAI...
...FOR ONE QUARTER OF THE TIME?!
B-BMP
B-BMP
B-BMP
B-BMP
B-BMP
EH?! W-WHAT?!
EH? EH? EH? EH? EH? EH? EH?
IT... CAN'T BE!
WHAT ARE WE GONNA DO?!
MASTERRRR!

Several years later...
CHIRA CHIRA
...
GUESS IT'S A NO-GO... AGAIN... THIS YEAR.
SEEMS THAT WAY...
CHIRA CHIRA
WELL...
WE'VE ARGUED ALL NIGHT WITHOUT CONSENSUS.
AND NOW, WE MUST ADJOURN INCONCLUSIVELY.
WE'LL HAVE TO REVISIT THE QUESTION OF WHETHER LORD RIKUO IS FIT TO BECOME THE THIRD SUPREME COMMANDER ON ANOTHER NIGHT...
SIGH
SHFF
URGHHH...
WILL NO ONE ENDORSE HIM?
WHAT CAN I SAY, SUPREME COMMANDER?
JUST LOOK.
JUST LOOK AT HIM.
TMP TMP

WELL, MOTHER...
I'M OFF!
YACK
YACK
Nura Rikuo
12 Years Old, 7th Grade
YOU'RE LEAVING ALREADY?
I HAVEN'T FINISHED MAKING YOUR LUNCH YET.
FLIP
FLOP
IT'S OKAY. I'LL BUY SOMETHING AT SCHOOL.
YACK
OH, MASTER!!
YACK
GOOD MORNING!!
I'LL PRE-PARE-
MORN-ING!
THAT'S OKAY. I CAN TAKE CARE OF IT!
WHY THE DEVIL DOESN'T HE TRANSFORM ANYMORE?
MUTTER
MUTTER
AFTER THAT ONE TIME, I THOUGHT HE'D BECOME A YOKAI FOR SURE, BUT...
AH!
TOK
TOK
MEETINGS AGAIN, GRANDPA?
UH... YES...
YOU'D BETTER NOT BE DREAMING UP EVIL SCHEMES!
AND BE NICE TO THE NEIGHBORS, OKAY?
ALL RIGHT THEN!
I'M OFF TO SCHOOL!
TIP
SLUMP
IF YOU ASK ME...
HE'S PERFECT. FOR A HUMAN, THAT IS...

WELL, YOKAI CAN'T DO MUCH DURING THE DAY, ANYWAY.
BUT... COME NIGHT-FALL...
SIGH
HOW LONG MUST I REMAIN SUPREME COMMANDER?
I WANT TO RETIRE AND ENJOY LIFE!
WHEN WILL RIKUO LIVE UP TO HIS RESPONSI-BILITIES AS THE THIRD?!

SEE YA!
INDEED... WHO KNOWS?

CHOK
CHOK
Is this deep enough, Master?
Yeah!
Thanks!
The day before...

Act 2: Rikuo Explores the School at Night

I HEARD THIS STORY FROM A FRIEND, SO I KNOW IT'S TRUE.
THERE'S AN OLD ABANDONED BUILDING HERE.
REALLY?
WHERE?
IT'S ON SCHOOL PROPERTY, BUT NOBODY'S ALLOWED TO GO THERE...
SKITTER SKITTER
...BECAUSE IT'S HAUNTED. BY GHOSTS AND GHOULS AND STUFF.
AND ANYBODY WHO GOES INSIDE...
...NEVER COMES OUT. EVER!
OH, COME ON!
ARE YOU SERIOUS?!
I CAN TELL YOU MORE...
...BUT ONLY IF YOU PROMISE... NEVER TO GO THERE.

Ukiyoe Town
Headquarters of the Nura Clan
CHIRP
CHIRP
SO?
WHY IS THAT MY PROBLEM?
THIS MAGAZINE IS ABOUT URBAN LEGENDS.
THIS ONE COVERS THE KAPPA.
ALL SORTS OF WEBSITES ARE TALKING ABOUT YOKAI!
SPORTS ATTACK
THE WORLD IS IN THE MIDST OF A YOKAI CRAZE!
HOW ARE YOU GOING TO TAKE RESPONSIBILITY FOR THIS?
...
LIKE I SAID...
...THIS YOKAI CRAZE... WHY IS IT MY PROBLEM?
SINCE YOU'RE SITTING AROUND THE HOUSE ALL DAY, SHIRKING YOUR DUTY AS THE THIRD...

...THOSE YOUNG, SMALL-TIME YOKAI ARE MAKING FOOLS OF US, WREAKING HAVOC IN OUR TERRITORY!
YOU WERE AMAZING THAT ONE TIME!
WHAT HAPPENED TO YOU?!
WHAT?
I LOST CONTROL. IT JUST HAPPENED!
I DON'T EVEN REMEMBER WHAT I DID!
THAT IS SO IRRESPONSIBLE!!
I REMEMBER IT, CLEAR AS NIGHT!!
YOU SAID, "FOLLOW ME," OR SOMETHING COOL LIKE THAT-
OI, RIKUO!
WHAT'S WITH ALL THE RUCKUS SO EARLY IN THE MORNING?
Yokai Supreme Commander Nurarihyon
THANKS TO YOUR "POLICY OF NON-INTERFERENCE," I'M GETTING YELLED AT.
WHAT CHOICE DO I HAVE?
JUST LOOK AT ME, I'M AN OLD MAN. YOU'D BETTER TAKE OVER SOON.
KOFF KOFF
MY TIME'S RUNNING OUT.
DON'T PULL THAT ACT!!
I SAW YOU PULL A DINE-AND-DASH YESTERDAY EVENING!!

I'VE DECIDED TO LIVE A HUMAN LIFE, OKAY?
I'M NOT GOING TO FOLLOW IN YOUR FOOTSTEPS, GRANDPA.
Cucumber
THANK YOU, MASTER!
BLURP
WAIT—ONLY ONE?!
YOU GET COVERED IN A MAGAZINE...
...AND SUDDENLY YOU'RE ACTING LIKE A CELEBRITY?
AT LEAST CARRY A SWORD WITH YOU, MASTER!
IT'S A DANGEROUS WORLD OUT THERE!
I'M FINE!! I'M JUST GOING TO SCHOOL!
BUT YOU'LL JUST GET BULLIED AGAIN!
EH?
TROMP
TROMP
WHAT?!
MASTER, IS SOMEONE BULLYING YOU?!
NO, NO...
I MAKE SURE NOBODY KNOWS THE TRUTH ABOUT ME.
MASTER, YOU'RE IMPORTANT TO US...
WE WON'T LET ANYONE HURT YOU.
I'LL MAKE THEM PAY!!
NO! PLEASE!
I'M BEGGING YOU! DON'T DO ANY "HAUNTING"!!

I'M HEADING OFF!!
HONESTLY... AND HERE I THOUGHT HE'D AWAKENED...
MUTTER
MUTTER
HE STILL REMAINS A HUMAN...
THAT EVENING SEEMS LIKE IT WAS JUST A DREAM...
MY, MY.
WILL LORD RIKUO EVER...
...ASSUME HIS RESPONSIBILITIES AS THE THIRD?
KAKLAK
KLAK
I'M NOT THE SAME PERSON I USED TO BE.
Front Station
Morning
I NEVER TALK ABOUT YOKAI AT SCHOOL ANYMORE!
I'M BECOMING AN UPSTANDING CITIZEN!
My home is filled with yokai...
...because my grandpa is their Supreme Commander.
HM...
I mentioned it at school once a few years back and caused a big stink.
I THINK I'M BEING FOLLOWED...
WSSH
COME ON, KARASU-TENGU! YOU'RE FOLLOWING ME TO SCHOOL, NOW?!

WHOA!
BN BN BN
R-RIKUO...?
WHAT THE...?!
KUH...
KANA?!
N-NO! I'M REALLY SORRY!!
ARE YOU TRYING TO KILL ME?!
HM... I DID SENSE SOMETHING, THOUGH...
SHFF
MORNING, NURA!!!
WHAT'S GOING ON?! FIGHTING FIRST THING IN THE MORNING?
DID YOU DO IT? THAT THING?
EHHH? WHAT THING?
AHH... NOW THIS IS WHAT A NORMAL MORNING FEELS LIKE!
JUST KIDDING.

TA-DA
Homework
OF COURSE!!
WOW! GREAT!
NOW. I HATE TO ASK, BUT...
AH!
NO PROBLEM!
BEAM
YAKI-SOBA SANDWICH AND A VEGETABLE JUICE, RIGHT?
I'M HAPPY TO HELP!! I'LL BE GLAD TO BUY YOU LUNCH!
AW, YOU REMEMBERED!
YOU'RE A GREAT GUY, NURA!
That's why I like you!
...
THAT WAS NICE OF HIM TO SAY.
I MADE HIM HAPPY.
YAMMER
THAT'S ...
...
SHEEN
I'M NOT DISLIKED ...
UP-STANDING CITIZEN
...WHICH MEANS...
...I'M THE COMPLETE OPPOSITE OF YOKAI...
...SO, THEY WON'T FIND OUT.
RIKUO... YOU'VE CHANGED.
OR, WERE YOU ALWAYS THIS WAY?
BRRING
AH! OH, NO!
I'M LATE! THAT'S WHAT I GET FOR TAKING A DIFFERENT ROUTE.

C'MON, NURA!
BRRRRRING
YOU DON'T COME THIS WAY EVERY DAY?
HEAD FOR THE BACK DOOR, BY THE SHOE LOCKERS...
IT'S CLOSER!
EH?
NEVER-MIND.
I'M TELLING YOU...
...YOKAI EXIST!
REALLY, KIYO-TSUGU?!
YACK
YACK
IS THIS SOME NEW RE-SEARCH?
WHAT? WHAT'S GOING ON?
YACK
IT'S KIYOTSUGU FROM THE OTHER CLASS. HE'S TALKING ABOUT YOKAI AGAIN.
HEE HEE
YACK
HE'S BEEN HUNTING THEM DURING LUNCH.
Y... YOKAI?
KIYOTSUGU?
THAT GUY?!

HOW CAN YOU BE SO SURE, MAN?
ACCORDING TO MY RESEARCH...
...IT'S DEFINITELY HARD TO SPOT OLD-FASHIONED, "TRADITIONAL" YOKAI.
THEY DON'T REALLY FIT IN OUR MODERN WORLD.
BUT!!
I ANALYZED THE REPORTS POSTED ON MY WEBSITE TO FIGURE OUT THE TRUTH!
HERE!
YOKAI NET
THERE WAS A REGIME CHANGE IN THE YOKAI WORLD.
TO THIS DAY, YOKAI ARE THE CULPRIT BEHIND ALL SORTS OF MISCHEIF.
EHH?!
TALK ABOUT A FLIP-FLOP...
HA HA HA... YOKAI DON'T EXIST.
EVERYONE'S GOING TO MAKE FUN OF YOU FOR SAYING THAT.
WOW!
WOW!
HE'S RIGHT!
SO SMART!
KIYOTSUGU IS SOOOO COOL! ♡
I forgive you for talking about weird stuff-♡
EHH?!
Even if I still don't believe you...
NURA, SORRY FOR MAKING FUN OF YOU BEFORE.
I'VE SEEN THE LIGHT...
HA HA HA...
...THANKS TO THAT GUY.
THAT GUY?

R M M B
YES. THAT GUY...
...THE YOUNG RULER OF THE DARK WORLD...
WHEN I WAS YOUNGER... HE RESCUED ME FROM EVIL.
COULD ...
COULD HE MEAN ...?
I'M IN LOVE!!
I'VE BEEN POSSESSED BY HIS SHADOWY CHARMS!
I JUST WANT TO MEET HIM AGAIN. THAT'S WHY I'M SEARCHING HIGH AND LOW FOR HIM!
DOM
UWAAAAAH!
THIS IS GETTING OUT OF HAND!
IF...IF THIS KEEPS UP, MY COVER WILL BE BLOWN!
YACK YACK
AHHH!
THAT GUY BACK THEN...
...
KIYOTSUGU?! YOU CAN'T MEAN...
THE RUMORED... ABANDONED SCHOOL BUILDING?!
YES... I'M GOING THERE.
EHHH?!
NO WAY... HOLD ON...
IT'S TOO DANGER-OUS!!

YAMMER
AND I WANT YOU ALL TO HELP!
SHIVER...
BUT IT WON'T BE EASY. SO I'M LOOKING FOR VOLUNTEERS!
UH... I HAVE SOMETHING TO DO TODAY!
M-ME TOO...
WHAT ABANDONED SCHOOL BUILDING?
HUH?!
YOU DON'T KNOW?!
FWIP
IT'S A CREEPY STORY ABOUT OUR SCHOOL!!
ABOUT YOKAI!!
LOOK! IT'S IN A MAGAZINE! IT'S FAMOUS!!
Urban Legend Special
?!
BUT...
THIS SCHOOL ISN'T THAT OLD!
WHOA!
TOK
TOK
TOK
TOK
Y'KNOW THE ROAD THAT RUNS RIGHT ALONG CAMPUS?
THE "EAST-CENTRAL HIGHWAY"?
WELL, ON THE OTHER SIDE OF IT, THERE'S AN OLD BUILDING.
AH...

V R R R M M M M
IT WAS CUT OFF WHEN THE ROAD CAME THROUGH.
NOBODY'S SET FOOT INSIDE FOR TEN YEARS OR MORE. THAT'S THE ABANDONED SCHOOL BUILDING.
YACK YACK
...
ALRIGHT... WE'RE ALL HERE.
ALL SIX OF US.
THIS'LL BE COOL, KIYOTSUGU!
AND NURA? YOU'RE AN HONORARY TEAM MEMBER!
...
DO US PROUD!
NOT COMING ...
...WOULD'VE BEEN THE SMART MOVE.
BUT WHEN I SAW THAT ARTICLE...
...I GOT A BAD FEELING ABOUT THE WHOLE THING.
Urban Legend Special
WHAT IF SOME OF OUR CLAN ARE IN THERE?

I'VE GOT TO GO CHECK IT OUT.
I CAN'T LET ANYTHING HAPPEN TO MY FRIENDS.
YACK
YACK
HUH?
D
M
KANA?!
I THOUGHT YOU HATED SCARY STUFF!
SH-SHUT UP! WHAT'S IT TO YOU?
YACK
BESIDES, WHY ARE YOU HERE, RIKUO?
YACK
EH?
HM ...?
OH, THANKS FOR COMING!
UH... WHAT ARE YOUR NAMES?
TSURARA OIKAWA!
I JUST LOVE STUFF LIKE THIS!
YOW
I'M SO GLAD YOU CAME!
...

I JUST LOVE STUFF LIKE THIS, TOO.
NAME'S KURATA.
TMP
O-OH... REALLY?!
I GUESS SOME PEOPLE DO LIKE THIS STUFF.
OKAY! HERE'S OUR ROUTE.
OLD BUILDING
STAIRS
EAST-CENTRAL HIGHWAY
SCHOOL GROUNDS
POND
CURRENT POSITION
Plan
THE FENCE IS TOO HIGH TO CLIMB, AND WE CAN'T SWIM THROUGH THE POND.
SO, WE'RE GOING TO CLIMB UP TO THE HIGHWAY, WAIT FOR A BREAK IN TRAFFIC, THEN GO FOR IT.
There are two lanes each way, so be careful!
YEAH!
THAT'S KIYOTSUGU FOR YA!!
THIS IS SO FUN!
B-BMP
B-BMP
WORRY
...
※DON'T EVER DO THIS, KIDS!
WOAH!
WATCH THE INCLINE! IT'S STEEP!
EVEN HUMANS DO "BAD" STUFF SOMETIMES!

UWAH! IT'S EVEN CREEPIER UP CLOSE!
IT DOESN'T LOOK LIKE ANYONE'S BEEN HERE FOR A LONG TIME.
KREEE
NOBODY'S BEEN HERE SINCE THE HIGHWAY CAME THROUGH.
...
WE HAVE TO CHECK EVERY-THING OUT.
IF WE FIND A YOKAI, THEY SHOULD BE ABLE TO PUT US IN TOUCH WITH *THAT GUY!*
...
...
FWSH FWSH

Art Studio
WELL, LET'S CHECK THIS ROOM FIRST.
...
TOK
TOK
WEIRD STATUE!
CREEPY!
HOLD ON! DON'T WANDER OFF ON ME, RIKUO!
...
OKAY ...
GLOM
THIS IS BAD... IF A YOKAI DOES SHOW UP...
...HOW WILL I DEAL WITH IT WITHOUT BLOWING MY COVER?
...
AH!
LOOK... AT...
...ME!
SLAM

NGH! NGH!
SKRITCH
SKRITCH
NNNGH!
?
TH- THEY'RE HERE!
TOMP TOMP
THEY'RE REALLY HERE.
JUST HANGING OUT...
HUH? DID YOU HEAR SOMETHING?
Y- YOU'RE IMAGINING IT!!
I DIDN'T HEAR A THING!
THEY'RE ALL OVER THIS PLACE!!
SKITTER
HM... THIS LOOKS LIKE THE PANTRY.
UWAH... SOUNDS NASTY, WHAT WITH ALL THE WATER.
WANNA CHECK IT OUT?
B-BMP B-BMP
DON'T!!
B-BMP
WAAAH!!
WHAT ARE YOU DOING, NURA?
S-SORRY!
DON'T FREAK ME OUT!
SAY... I'M GETTING THIRSTY...
SKRI
SKRI
...

THUM
BLOOD ...
THUM
THUM
SO... THIRSTY ...
WANT... DRINK BLOOD ...
THUM
THUM
THUM
SLAM
IT'S ...
IT'S ANOTHER ONE...
WHAT A WEIRDO.
LET'S GO.
AHH!! WAIT!!
CHAMP
I'LL GO FIRST!
YAAAH!
TP TP TP TP
SLUP
BLUP
DOMP DOMP
NNGH!
WAAAAAH
FWUP
HAVE YOU LOST IT, NURA?
SLAM-MING DOORS
Rikuo! Wait up!
AHH!
AHH!

NOTHING HERE, HUH?
KIND OF A LET-DOWN...
NO WAY!
I CAN'T GET THEM ALL MYSELF.
IT ISN'T ABOUT MY COVER ANYMORE...
...
!
I'VE GOT TO DO SOMETHING, OR THEY'LL GET HURT.
I GUESS THIS IS OUR LAST STOP.
THE CAFETERIA.
AGH!!
W-WAIT!
HEY... THIS LOOKS PROMISING.
ZSH
ZSH
FEELS LIKE SOMETHING COULD POP OUT ANY-TIME...
EH?
CHOMP
CHOMP

NOM NOM
?
HHM...
...
...
EH?
...GUH...
GROSS!!

FWISHHH
GRRAAHHHHH!
...
TP TP TP TP TP TP
UWAH... AHHHH-HH!!
WHAT THE-?!
RIKUO--?!
TH-THEY'RE COMING!!
OH NO! WHAT SHOULD I DO?!
NOT GONNA MAKE IT!
LORD RIKUO...
DIDN'T WE TELL YOU?

EH?
JUST LIKE THIS, THESE LOW-LIFES...
...HAVE SET UP SHOP IN NURA TERRITORY!

LISTEN UP!
THIS ISN'T YOUR TERRITORY...
...YOU PUNKS!
MASTER, PULL YOURSELF TOGETHER!
WE NEED YOU TO BECOME THE THIRD!
...
EH?
W-WHAT ...?
W-WHAT'S GOING ON?!
YOU... WERE STUDENTS ...
WHA ?!
WE'RE YOUR "ESCORTS."
JUST LIKE KARASU-TENGU TOLD YOU.
EVER SINCE THAT DAY FOUR YEARS AGO...
...WE'VE BEEN WATCHING OVER YOU!
DIDN'T YOU REALIZE IT?!
WE'VE BEEN WITH YOU EVERY SINGLE DAY!

GASP
EVERY SINGLE DAY?!
WHA?!
I NEVER... I NEVER HEARD ABOUT THAT!!
NOT TRUE. YOU WERE TOLD.
IN FACT, I TOLD YOU MYSELF.
YAH!
B-BMP
FLAP FLAP
I'm going to make sure you have an escort!
AND MAY I EXPRESS MY DISAPPOINTMENT...
...THAT THE FUTURE SUPREME COMMANDER HAD SO MUCH TROUBLE DEALING WITH SUCH PUNY YOKAI!
I TOLD YOU, I'M HUMAN!
RAAAA
WAAA
ARE YOU STILL GOING ON ABOUT THAT?!
YOU POSSESS A QUARTER OF THE SUPREME COMMANDER'S BLOODLINE!
I JUST WANNA LIVE IN PEACE!
R-RIKUO? WHAT'S GOING ON?
HEY, CAN I... OPEN MY EYES YET?!
IS IT STILL SCARY?!
GLOM
EH?!
UH... JUST A BIT LONGER...
FAINTED
...

Uwaah! They really were there every day!
GASP
Tee hee!
Field day
School trip
Album

Act 3: The Anger of Rikuo's Sworn Brother

Act 3: The Anger of Rikuo's Sworn Brother

WHAT?!
I'M HOME!
YAMMER
WELCOME HOME, MASTER!
NOM
NOM
CRUNCH CRUNCH
OM
GOM
CANDY
...
THAT LOOKS LIKE VERY EXPENSIVE CANDY...
YEP!
AH
GRANDPA!
DON'T TELL ME YOU STOLE THAT!
FWUP
YOU SAID YOU'D EASE UP ON THE SHENANIGANS!!
DM
THE MORE TROUBLE YOU CAUSE HUMANS...
...THE MORE TROUBLE I'LL HAVE WITH THEM!
YOU HAVE IT ALL WRONG, LORD RIKUO.
YACK
IT WAS A GIFT.
THE ZEN GROUP CAME TO VISIT!

EH?
TIK TOK
SHA
MASTER!
LONG TIME, NO SEE!
IT'S ME, ZEN!
Head of the Zen Group
Zen
L-LORD ZEN!!
IT'S... IT'S BEEN YEARS!
HA HA! WHAT'S WITH THE "LORD"?
JUST CALL ME "ZEN."
WA HA HA
TIK TOK
...
HE MUST BE HERE FOR A REASON...
B-BMP B-BMP

WHAT'S HE DOING HERE?
WHAT BUSINESS DOES HE HAVE WITH MASTER?
THE HEAD OF THE ZEN GROUP AND THE MASTER USED TO PLAY AS CHILDREN.
WHISPER
WHISPER
THEY MUST HAVE A LOT TO TALK ABOUT.
...
HEY! ALL OF YOU, PIPE DOWN!
S-SORRY. I KEEP TELLING THEM...
...NOT TO BOTHER PEOPLE.
ALWAYS FULL OF ENERGY.
JUST WHAT I'D EXPECT FROM THE HEAD FAMILY.
YACK
I'LL CARRY IT!
NO! THAT'S MY JOB!
YACK
MASTER! I BROUGHT TEA!
WSSH
DOMP
WAH!
OW!!
I-I'M SO SORRY!
GRRAAAAH!
WHAT DO YOU THINK YOU'RE DOING, YOU DUMB BROAD?!

DOOM
THAT'S LORD RIKUO, MY SWORN BROTHER!!
I OUGHTA KILL YOU FOR THAT!!
GASP
PLOP
YOU'RE STILL THE SAME, MASTER...
FELL PREY TO ONE OF YOUR OWN PRANKS, EH?
NOT GOOD...
I GOTTA WATCH IT AROUND HIM...
UH... NO...
WHAT'S WITH THAT GUY?
WHISPER
WHAT A HOT-HEAD!
BOW
I WANTED TO APOLOGIZE FOR NOT MAKING THE BIG MEETING.
HUH? THAT? NO PROBLEM!
ALL THEY DO IS BRAG ABOUT THEIR LATEST EVIL DEEDS, ANYWAY.
WHAT? I CAN'T BELIEVE MY EARS!
YOU CAN'T TALK LIKE THAT, MASTER!
GRIN
BECAUSE...
...SOMEDAY, YOU'RE GOING TO LEAD ALL YOKAI!!
EH?
RMB
UWAH...

WHISPER
THERE SEEMS TO BE A MISUNDERSTANDING HERE...
WHISPER
WELL, IT HAS BEEN FIVE YEARS.
HA HA HA
AND, I'M REALLY, REALLY LOOKING FORWARD TO SEEING YOU BECOME THE THIRD SUPREME COMMANDER!
HA HA HA HA HA HA
HA HA HA
OH, STOP IT. YOU'VE GOT IT ALL WRONG...
I'M REMAINING HUMAN.
SHWM
STOP YANKING MY CHAIN!!
FWUMP
UM... EHH...
LISTEN UP, RIKUO!
THANKS TO YOUR WAFFLING, NOBODY CAN GET ENOUGH VOTES TO BECOME THIRD!
FUME
YOU KNEW?
FUME
FUME
OF COURSE!!
AND NOW, YOU'RE GONNA EXPLAIN WHY!
B-BUT... HOW CAN A HUMAN COMMAND YOKAI?
THERE'S NO WAY I COULD PULL IT OFF!

SOMEONE KILL THIS IDIOT FOR ME!!
UWAH!! S-SOME-ONE HELP!!
KYAAH!
WHOA!
MASTER RIKUO!
WHEN DID YOU GO SOFT ?!
DAMN IT!! IN THAT CASE...
...THERE'S NO REASON FOR ME TO CLING TO LIFE!!
BAH! I'M LEAVING!
KOFF KOFF
ARE YOU OKAY ?!
Z-ZEN?
DAMN IT... STAY BACK, YOU FOOL!
KOFF ...
KOFF ...
OI! SOME-ONE...
EH?!
HACK
YOU'RE BLEED-ING!

ZEN IS A BIRD YOKAI. HIS POWER IS IN HIS FEATHERS, WHICH TRANSFORM INTO A POWERFUL ORGANIC *POISON* WHEN SOAKED IN ALCOHOL.
HIS CLAN, THE ZEN GROUP, HARNESSES THE POWER OF MEDICINES AND POISONS.
BUT, ANY MEDICINE BECOMES A POISON IF USED FOR TOO LONG...
IT IS SAID THAT ZEN WAS BORN IN THE FORM OF A BEAUTIFUL BIRD.
BUT, AS HE REACHES MANHOOD, HIS FEATHERS BEGIN TURNING TO POISON, *SLOWLY KILLING* HIM.
THIS CHARACTERISTIC MAKES THE ZEN LINE PHYSICALLY WEAK. HE COULD PASS AWAY AT ANY TIME.
REALLY, HE'S A FRAGILE SORT OF YOKAI.
SIGH
IT'S BEEN A LONG TIME SINCE ZEN CAME TO VISIT.
WHY'D HE COME TODAY?
MAYBE IT WAS...
JOLT
...BECAUSE HE WAS SUMMONED!! BY YOU, GRANDPA!!
TO LECTURE ME!!
HMPH...
TSK
SO WHAT IF I DID?!
SO, IT *WAS* YOU, SUPREME COMMANDER!
GASP

WHAT WERE YOU THINKING? YOU KNOW ZEN'S HEALTH IS FRAGILE!
YOU'RE TERRI-BLE!
TERRIBLE, HUH?
HUMPH.
IF YOU REALLY FEEL THAT WAY, THEN TAKE OVER THE NURA SYNDICATE.
SLAM
HOW MANY TIMES DO I HAVE TO REPEAT MYSELF?!
LORD RIKUO. YOUR DAY STUDIES ARE IMPORTANT ...
...BUT I IMPLORE YOU TO REMEMBER YOUR "NIGHT STUDIES" AS WELL!
AND WHAT'S THIS ABOUT A SYNDICATE?!
IT'S JUST A GANG OF YOKAI WHO DO BAD STUFF!
LORD RIKUO.
THAT IS INCORRECT.
I IMPLORE YOU TO LEARN MORE ABOUT US.
NATTO-KOZO! BRING THE NURA CLAN'S "NIGHT PARADE" SCROLL.
AT ONCE!
PITTER PATTER

?
A MAP OF JAPAN?
READY?
THIS IS THE NURA CLAN SYNDICATE.
BENEATH THE HEAD FAMILY ARE MANY FRANCHISES.
A MAP OF OUR TERRITORY.
Daruma Group
Nura Clan Syndicate
Zen Group
FOR INSTANCE, LORD MOKUGYO-DARUMA'S "DARUMA GROUP," OR LORD ZEN'S "ZEN GROUP."
SINCE TIMES OF OLD, JAPAN HAS BEEN FILLED WITH YOKAI.
THOSE OF THE SEAS OR MOUNTAINS... HUMANOID, ANIMAL AND ARTIFACT... MOST DWELLING IN DARKNESS AND SHADOW. MOST QUITE WEAK.
WEAK ENOUGH TO REQUIRE PROTECTION, AND THIS IS ONE OF THE MAIN FUNC-TIONS OF THE NURA SYNDICATE.
IF YOU DO NOT TAKE UP THAT RESPONSIBILITY FOR THEM, LORD RIKUO, THEN WHO WILL?
...

KLATTA
KLATTA
...LORD ZEN?
HOW ARE YOU FEELING...
HE REALLY ISSS AN IDIOT...
...THAT HEIR TO THE NURA SSSYNDICATE.
TRAVELING ALL THISSS WAY, IN YOUR CONDITION!
LET USSS LEAVE THEM!
YOU DON'T NEED THE NURA CLAN, LORD ZEN!
I APPRECIATE THAT.
BUT JUST BETWEEN US, HEBIDAYU...
...MY TIME IS RUNNING OUT. FAST.
EH?!
MY FATHER AND HIS FATHER BEFORE HIM WERE FRAGILE, TOO.
AND THE CLAN PROTECTED US.
PLUS, WE HAVE LORD NURARIHYON TO THANK FOR OUR TERRITORY.
THAT'S WHY I'M HAPPY WE CAME, EVEN THOUGH MY TIME MAY BE SHORT...
THIS MUSHROOM IS POISONOUS.
THIS LEAF WILL MAKE YOU NAUSEOUS.
...AND I'M HAPPY TO BE OF SERVICE TO THE NURA CLAN.
WOW!
YOU KNOW SO MUCH, ZEN!

IT'S BECAUSE I SPECIALIZE IN POISONS.
YOKAI ARE SO COOL!!
WHEN I GROW UP, I'M GONNA BE A YOKAI!
AND I'M GONNA BE THE NEXT SUPREME COMMANDER!
...
BUT NOW, I'VE LIVED UP TO MY OBLIGATIONS.
I'M DONE.
THE SUPREME COMMANDER IS IN HIS TWILIGHT YEARS. I SUSPECT THE NURA SYNDICATE WON'T LAST LONG.
DID YOU HEAR?
I DID.
GUESS IT'S ALL OVER...
ZEN IS ABOUT TO DIE.
THERE'S NOTHING TO FEAR ANYMORE.
IF WE ARE TO STRIKE, NOW IS THE TIME...

TA-DA
CHECK IT OUT, KURO-TABO!!
WHERE'D YOU FIND THE SAKE?!
IN THE KITCHEN!
ALL PACKED UP IN A NICE WOODEN BOX!
WA HA HA
THIS IS "YO-SHU," HAUNTED WINE!
LET'S DRINK UP!
HEY, YOU GUYS!
FWAP
EH?!
IS THAT YOURS, MASTER?
DO YOU DRINK?!
NO, IT'S AN APOLOGY GIFT FOR ZEN!
HE WAS FORCED TO COME ALL THIS WAY AND THAT WAS WRONG!
MASTER ...
I'VE GOT TO EXPLAIN THINGS...
...ABOUT HOW I'M HUMAN!
I KNOW HE'LL UNDER-STAND ...
...ABOUT WHY I CAN'T INHERIT THE CLAN!
IT'S ALREADY TOO LATE...
BUT, I'D BETTER GO ALONG...
...TO SEE IF I CAN KEEP LORD ZEN FROM LOSING IT.

KAW KAW
ANYONE KNOW WHICH WAY THEY WENT?
EH?! I'VE GOT TO TAKE THE GLOOM CART?!
I'M GOING AS WELL. IT'S GETTING DARK.
YOU ARE ...?
HEBIDAYU. I'M GOING OUT FOR SOME SHOP—
HM?
WHAT THE...? IT'S DEAD QUIET...
AND NOBODY'S HERE?!
MY THROAT'S DRY... ...AND IT FEELS HOT.
!
KRAK KRAK
FOOOOOOOM
?!
EVERYONE'S SSSAFELY OUT... I SSSAW TO THAT...
HSSS

FUOOOM
HEBIDAYU?!
WHAT HAVE YOU DONE?!
I CAN'T BELIEVE...
YOU BE-TRAYED ME!
SHING
SO MUCH FOR LOYALTY.
KOFF
LOYALTY?! WHAT ARE YOU TALKING ABOUT?
ACTING ASSS YOUR SSSERVANT WASSS BUT A MEANSSS TO AN END...
...AND THAT END WASSS BUILDING MY OWN GANG.
HA HA HA...
PATHETIC.
YOU CALL YOURSSSELF A YOKAI?!
YOU'RE JUSSST A LITTLE BIRD!
FWSSSHH
AND NOW YOU'RE GONNA DIE LIKE ONE!!

...
WE'RE HERE, MASTER.
O-OKAY...
...?
FEATHERS ?
...
MASTER!
?!
FOOOOOM
LORD ZEN'S MANSION... IT'S AFLAME!
WHAT WOULD YOU HAVE ME DO?!
WHAT?!
...
T-TAKE US IN!!
EH ?!
WHY ?
NEVER MIND! POWER US STRAIGHT IN!!
EHH ?!

WHAT?
WHAT HAPPENED?!
THE GLOOM CART?! THE SSSYNDICATE!! HOW DID THEY...?
ZEN?!
BM
FOOOF
KOFF...
HANG IN THERE!!

R-RIKUO...
W-WHAT ARE YOU DOING...
... HERE?
WHO?!
?!
IT'S THAT FOOLISSSH NURA BOY!
WHY'D YOU COME?
I CAN'T PROTECT YOU HERE!
KARASU-TENGU. WHO ARE THESE GUYS?
I DON'T KNOW. I THOUGHT THEY WERE ZEN GROUP HIGHER-UPS...
HEHE... YOU'RE RIGHT...
THERE'SSS DISSSENT IN THE EXECUTIVE RANKSSS...
WE WANT NURARI-HYON'SSS GRANDSS-SON OUT.
HSSSSSSSS
AND NOW, I'LL TAKE HIM OUT TO SSSTAKE MY CLAIM!
SHUT YOUR TRAP.
R-RIKUO!! LEAVE NOW!
YOU CAN'T DO ANYTHING HERE!

STAY BACK.
GAH!
!!
?!

SPLUT
SPLUT
SPLUT
SPLUT
OH!
OOOH!
WHAT IS HE?!
R-RUN!!
FLEE!
...
WHO... ARE YOU?
LORD RIKUO ...
...HAS AWAKENED ONCE AGAIN.
RIKUO?!
HE'S RIKUO?!

HEY, ZEN.
IT'S THE FIRST TIME WE'VE MET... LIKE THIS.
I SEE...
SO, YOU'RE ONE-QUARTER YOKAI.
I'M PATHETIC.
I'M SUPPOSED TO BE A FULL-FLEDGED YOKAI.
BUT IN THE END, I NEEDED RESCUING.
KOFF
KOFF
RIKUO, CONSIDERING WHO YOU ARE NOW, ARE YOU GONNA DO IT?
WILL YOU BE THE THIRD?

BEFORE I DIE...
...DO SOMETHING THAT'LL MAKE ME HAPPY.
WANNA DRINK?
...
YOU'RE GIVING ME SAKE NOW?
YEAH.
PASS ME YOUR CUP.
I'LL FORMALLY PLEDGE MY ALLEGIANCE HERE AND NOW.
I MAY BE DYING...
...BUT I'M PROUD TO BE BROTHERS IN THE SAME CLAN.
NOT FROM YOUR GRANDFATHER'S GENERATION, BUT FROM YOURS.
YOU GOT IT.
YOU'RE ONE FRAGILE YOKAI, ZEN.

AND I'LL PROTECT YOU.
HA HA HA... YOU'RE A STRAIGHT TALKER IN YOUR NIGHT-FORM, RIKUO.
IT'S A SHAME, BUT...
...WHEN DAWN BREAKS, HE'LL PROBABLY RETURN TO NORMAL.
IF ONLY...
...WE COULD SHOW THE CLAN HEADS THIS VERSION OF HIM, THEY'D BE SATISFIED.
KARASU...
...
YES?

HOW MANY MORE CUPS OF SAKE DO I NEED TO DRINK...
...FOR THE OTHER YOKAI TO ACCEPT ME?
WHAT?!
I'M GOING TO BECOME THE THIRD.
THIS... THIS MAN....
...IS SO DIFFERENT FROM THE BOY.
WHAT DOES IT MEAN?
HEY... THAT MAP.
THAT MAP YOU SHOWED ME.
HOW MANY CLAN HEADS ARE THERE, IN ALL?

鴫
Zen
Ah...!
Better not...
...
PLOP

Act 4: Rikuo's Dream
IT'S THE SAKURA TREE IN OUR YARD...
SOMETHING'S NOT RIGHT...
SPRING PASSED A LONG TIME AGO...
WHO'S THERE?
SOMEONE'S THERE...
WHO IS IT?

Act 4:
Rikuo's Dream

CHIRP
CHIRP
TA
DA
GOOD MORNING, MASTER!!
BLING
BLING
BLING
...
UM...
WHAT'S THIS?
I WAS SO TOUCHED, MASTER.
YOU TRUELY REALIZED THE GLORY OF THE NURA CLAN.
TWINKLE
A NEW ERA BEGINS! I SHALL REMEMBER IT ALWAYS!
WELL—
—I'D SAY YOUR BRAVERY LAST NIGHT DESERVES A REWARD.
EH?
HEY, KARASU.
SHF
SHF
WE HEARD THE MASTER HAS AWAKENED!!

BM
I'M SO HAPPY.
AND THAT HE ANNOUNCED HIS INTENTION TO BECOME THIRD!
BM
THUMP
AND THAT HE TRANSFORMED AGAIN!
YACK
I'M SO TOUCHED! I HAVE LUMPS IN MY THROATS!
YACK
THIS IS A GLORIOUS MOMENT FOR THE FAMILY!
YACK
LET THE CELEBRATION BEGIN!
W-WAIT A MINUTE!!
WHAT ARE YOU TALKING ABOUT?
...HUH?
I HAVE NO IDEA WHAT YOU'RE TALKING ABOUT...
I DON'T REMEMBER A THING.
...WHAT?!
RIGHT, MASTER?
SHUP
YAMMER
TELL US, KARASU-TENGU!!
OH, I WISH YOU COULD HAVE SEEN HIM!
TOMP
IF THE CLAN HEADS HAD BEEN THERE, THE DECISION WOULD BE FINAL!
LAST NIGHT, YOU TRANSFORMED YET AGAIN...
MY, YOU WERE GLORIOUS. SO GALLANT!
HA HA HA! YOU'RE SUCH A KIDDER!

MASTER! PLEASE TELL US YOU'RE KIDDING! PLEASE!
YOU WANNA PARTY THIS EARLY IN THE MORNING? COUNT ME OUT.
What's with these guys?
FOR SOME REASON, I FEEL LIKE I DIDN'T SLEEP WELL LAST NIGHT.
I DID HAVE THE STRANGEST DREAM, THOUGH.
WHO WAS THAT?
COME TO THINK OF IT, I DON'T REMEMBER ANYTHING AFTER ARRIVING AT ZEN'S HOUSE.
MAYBE I DID TRANSFORM?
HUH?
MY LEGS ARE ALL WOBBLY, TOO!
HIC!
WOBBLE...
YACK
YACK
KANA!
GOOD MORN-ING!
MORNING. WE'RE EARLY TODAY!
WHEW
THIS IS GREAT.
SEEING KANA HERE HELPS ME FORGET HOW WEIRD MY HOME LIFE IS.

GLOOO—OM
YO.
HAVEN'T SEEN YOU IN A WHILE...
NOT SINCE OUR LITTLE ADVENTURE...
KI...
KIYO-TSUGU?!
YOU GUYS...
...SAW THEM, RIGHT? RIGHT?!
S-SAW WHO?
YOU KNOW!
THEM!
THEY MUST'VE BEEN THERE... IN THE OLD SCHOOL BUILDING.
THAT'S THE REASON WE WENT. THE YOKAI I WAS HUNTING!!
BUT, WHEN I WOKE UP, I WAS LYING ON A PARK BENCH...
GRA—AH
NURA! TELL ME YOU SAW SOMETHING!! ANYTHING!!
THWUP THWUP
NNGH... GACK...
N-NOTHING!
KOFF KOFF
STRANGE...
I KNOW THEY WERE THERE!

MAYBE YOU'RE CONFUSING THEM WITH THOSE DELINQUENTS?
REMEMBER THOSE BAD KIDS WHO WERE HANGING OUT THERE? THEY TRIED TO SCARE US.
OH, I REMEMBER YOU!
IS THAT WHAT HAPPENED?
YUKI-ONNA?!
YEP!
WAIT... DON'T TELL ME YOU FAINTED?
HOW EMBARRASSING...
N-NO WAY!
OF COURSE NOT!! I DIDN'T FAINT!!
D-DELINQUENTS, RIGHT. DELINQUENTS!!
A WHOLE GANG OF 'EM...
YEP! YOKAI WOULD NEVER JUST SHOW UP AT SCHOOL LIKE THAT!
...
YAK
HA HA HA
Yeah, that's what happened...
YAK
H-HOLD ON...
UM...
MASTER!!
YOU CAN'T JUST GO OFF TO SCHOOL ALONE!
Not anymore!!
OH, AND HERE'S LUNCH FROM YOUR MOTHER!!
FWIP
BRRRR!

VOOOO
RRRMMMBB
WHAT'S WRONG?
WHAT ARE YOU DOING HERE?
WATCHING OVER YOU, MASTER!
I WANT MY SCHOOL LIFE TO BE PEACEFUL!!
IF ANYONE FINDS OUT, I'M DEAD!
BUT IT'S ORDERS...
AT LEAST STOP CALLING ME "MASTER"!
THEN PLEASE CALL ME "OIKAWA" OR "TSURARA."
EH?!
...
IT'S THAT GIRL FROM BEFORE.
MAYBE SHE'S A FRIEND OF RIKUO'S?
NO... HE SURE ISN'T ACTING LIKE IT.
ON THE OTHER HAND, SHE BROUGHT HIM LUNCH...
WHAT'S THAT ALL ABOUT?
...
I GUESS THERE'S A LOT I DON'T KNOW ABOUT RIKUO...
EXCUSE ME...

COULD YOU TELL ME WHERE THE OFFICE IS?
I'M LOST...
AH. IT'S ON THE SECOND FLOOR.
BEAM
THANKS.
?
HER ACCENT...
IS SHE A TRANSFER STUDENT?
BRRRING
RING
RING
I'M FROM KYOTO.
MY NAME'S KEIKAIN.

MURMUR MURMUR
YURA KEIKAIN...
PLEASED TO MEET YOU.
KEIKAIN!! WHERE DID YOU MOVE FROM?
YACK
"KEIKAIN" IS HARD TO SAY!
CAN I CALL YOU "YURA"?
YACK
WHAT CLUBS ARE YOU GOING TO JOIN?
YACK
YACK
WELL, I WAS THINKING...
YACK
TELL US ABOUT IT, KIYOTSUGU!
YACK
SERIOUSLY? YOU WENT TO THE ABANDONED SCHOOL-HOUSE?
W-WELL...
YACK
SEE ANY YOKAI?!
WHAT?! YOU DID?!

NO...
NONE AT ALL...
REALLY?
WHAT A LET-DOWN.
URK...
W-WAIT!
NEXT TIME!!
I'LL FIND THEM NEXT TIME! LISTEN!!
HERE WE GO AGAIN.
YEAH...
HE NEVER GIVES UP...
I BOUGHT A CURSED DOLL AND A DIARY FROM SOME PARANORMAL RESEARCH FANATICS I KNOW IN TOWN!!
EH?!
AND I'M GOING TO USE THEM TO PROVE MY THEORY ONCE AND FOR ALL!!
BAM
EH?!
EH?!
THAT STORY...
...IS IT TRUE?
I'D LOVE TO SEE!
EH?!
R...
REALLY?!

HOLD ON, YURA...
WHISPER
SO THAT'S WHAT SHE'S INTO.
WHISPER
WOW! I'M SO DELIGHTED YOU'RE INTERESTED.
IS THAT UNUSUAL?
NO, NOT AT ALL!!
I HAVE OTHER INTREPID FRIENDS TOO!!
LIKE TORII AND MAKI RIGHT HERE!
WHP
EH?!
ME?!
OOH, MY STOMACH ...
I HAVE A HEAD-ACHE...
Ah-ha!
IENAGA!! NURA!! GREAT TIMING!!
GEH!
MAN ...
ALL RIGHT!! I'M ON A ROLL, NOW!!
WE ARE NOW THE KIYOJUJI PARANORMAL PATROL!!
WOO HOO
GACK!
What an awful name...
LET'S HAVE OUR FIRST MEETING AT MY HOUSE TONIGHT!!
WHO ASKED HIM TO FORM A CLUB?

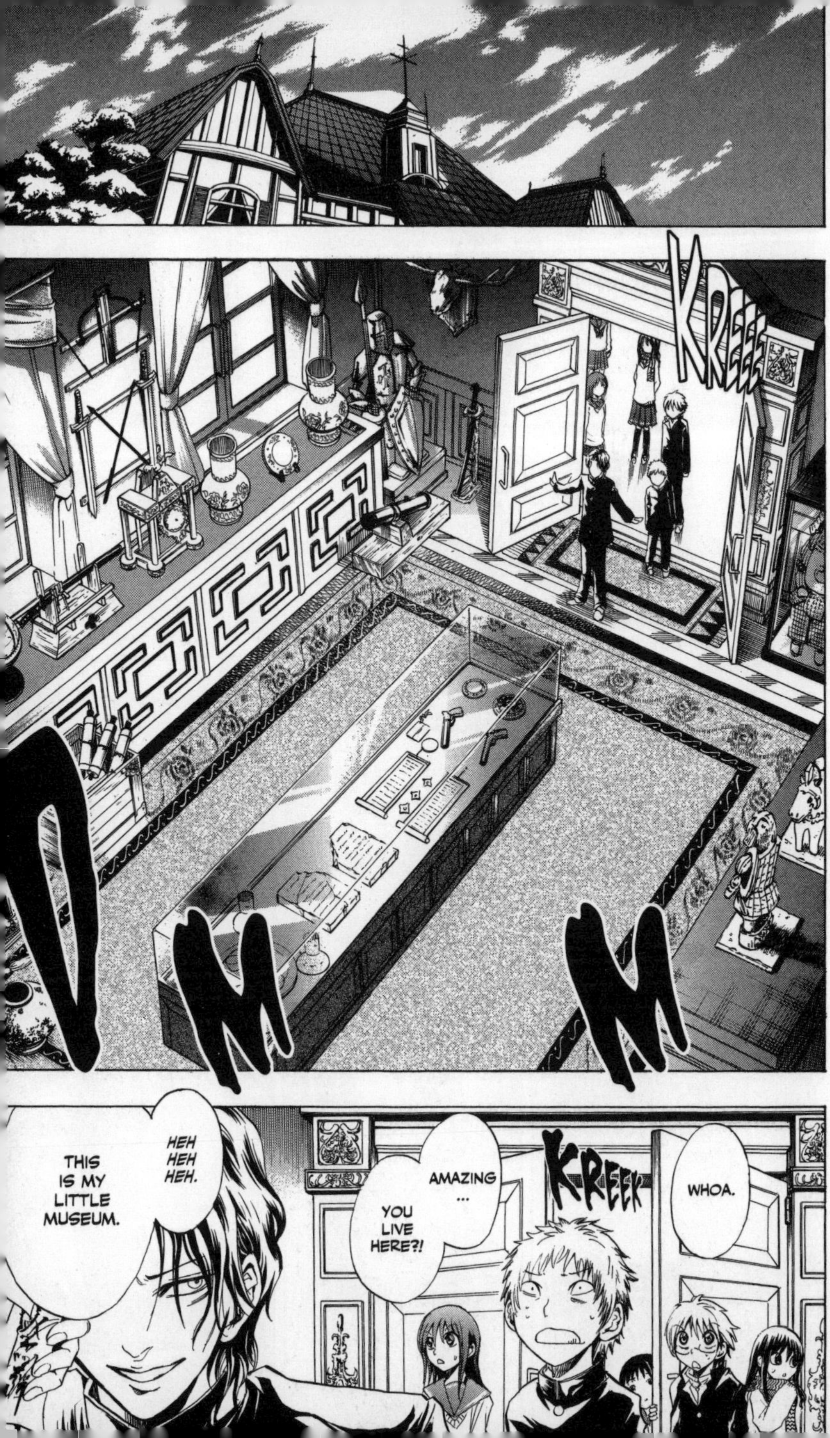
KREEE
D M M
WHOA.
KREEK
AMAZING ...
YOU LIVE HERE?!
HEH HEH HEH.
THIS IS MY LITTLE MUSEUM.

ARE YOUR PARENTS NEWLY RICH OR SOMETHING?
BITE YOUR TONGUE!!
MY GRANDFATHER WAS A UNIVERSITY PROFESSOR. I'M JUST BORROWING HIS OFFICE.
ALTHOUGH... I SORT OF FILLED IT UP WITH MY OWN THINGS.
WOW!
YOU SURE HAVE A LOT OF COOL STUFF...
HOW THE HECK DID HE GET ALL THIS?
YUKI-ONNA... I MEAN, TSURARA!
ARE THERE ANY YOKAI IN OUR CLAN WHO CAN POSSESS OBJECTS?
THIS WAY.
...
WELL... YOU MEAN ONES WHO INHABIT DOLLS? NO.
BUT, WE DO HAVE SOME WHO INHABIT ARTIFACTS. MODERN ONES.
I HAVE THAT BAD FEELING AGAIN...
THIS IS SO CLOSE TO HOME, TOO.
?
IF ANYTHING SHOWS UP, JUST TRANSFORM AGAIN AND TAKE 'EM OUT!
NO WAY!! I CAN'T DO THAT!!
...
They're at it again...

IT'S THIS JAPANESE DOLL...
OOOH...
YEAH. IT'S LIKE YOU SAID.
IS IT REALLY CURSED?
I'M PRETTY CERTAIN IT IS.
IT CAME WITH THE PREVIOUS OWNER'S DIARY.
DIARY?
LET ME READ AN EXCERPT.
SWIP
"FEBRUARY 22ND... JUST ONE WEEK UNTIL THE MOVERS COME.
"I STARTED CLEANING YESTERDAY, AND USED THE OPPORTUNITY TO THROW OUT THE OLD DOLL THAT GRANDMA GAVE ME.
"I'D BEEN WAITING FOR A CHANCE TO DO THAT. I JUST COULDN'T BRING MYSELF TO TOSS IT EARLIER. I WAS TOO *SCARED*.
"IT WAS POURING RAIN, BUT I TOOK IT OUTSIDE ANYWAY...
FWIP

"BUT WHEN I WOKE UP THIS MORNING, I FOUND IT IN THE FRONT HALL! JET-BLACK BLOOD WAS DRIPPING FROM ITS EYES!"
THOMP
WHAT'S WRONG WITH YOU, RIKUO?!
DON'T YOU TACKLE MY PRECIOUS RESEARCH MATERIAL!!
HA HA...
MY APOLOGIES, I JUST FELT SO SORRY FOR IT!
WIPE WIPE
ARE YOU INSANE?!
MASTER?
URGH! THIS LOOKS LIKE IT'S THE REAL DEAL!
Not again...
HOLD ON! LET ME SEE THAT!!

...
GOOD. IT'S OKAY.
YOU'D BETTER WATCH IT...
...OR YOU'LL LOSE YOUR HONORED MEMBER STATUS...
ANYWAY... LET'S CONTINUE.
...
"FEBRUARY 24TH. I ASKED MY BOYFRIEND TO TAKE IT INTO THE MOUNTAINS AND GET RID OF IT.
"THAT NIGHT, I GOT A CALL. 'HELP! I THREW IT OUT, *BUT NOW IT'S BACK IN MY HOUSE!*'"
EH?
A-AND, WHAT HAPPENS NEXT?
"NOW THAT I THINK BACK, THERE'S ALWAYS BEEN SOMETHING *STRANGE* ABOUT THAT DOLL.
"SOMETIMES IT SEEMED AS THOUGH ITS HAIR *STARTED GROWING...*"
FWMM
FWMM
FWMM
AH! MASTER, IT'S...
YEAH. NOT GOOD.
I'LL FREEZE IT!
D-DON'T! NOT IN FRONT OF EVERYONE...
"FEBRUARY 28TH. THE DAY BEFORE MOVING DAY.

"IT'S SO STRANGE. THE BOX I PACKED IS OPEN, AND..."
THE DIARY!
STOP READING THE DIARY!!
BS

?!
I KNEW IT WAS HERE...
IN THE NAME OF THE KEIKAIN ONMYOJI CLAN...
...YOKAI, I DISPATCH THEE FROM THIS WORLD!

Setting: *Ukiyoe Town Middle School classroom. Chalkboard: Kiyojuji Paranormal Patrol, Yokai Meeting #360. (Sounds of chatter)*

KIYOTSUGU: We're all here! Let's begin.

SHIMA: Who else but Kiyotsugu could set up a club so quickly?

YURA: Even if there are only three members.

KIYOTSUGU: Never fear, Keikain! We're growing every day. Let's kick off today's meeting. First order of business: a debriefing of the events that occurred at the abandoned school building the other day.

SHIMA: Man, that was scary. I never expected to run into real yokai.

YURA: *(gulp)* Tell me more.

KIYOTSUGU: I think you're mixed up there, Shima. Oikawa, who was with us, swears that they were just juvenile delinquents. Though they did smell pretty bad, even for a group of thugs.

SHIMA: Who? Oikawa? Oh, wait. The one with the scarf, right? Yeah.

KIYOTSUGU: She doesn't exactly dress for the season, does she? Anyway, on to the topic at hand: yokai!

SHIMA: What, we're not talking about Oikawa anymore? Uh, I mean, not that I care or anything...

KIYOTSUGU: What's with this fixation on Oikawa all of a sudden? Wait a second. Don't tell me...

SHIMA: Whoa! No! It's nothing! It's not like I think she's really, really cute or anything!

YURA: *(under breath)* Who cares! Let's just get on with the discussion...

KIYOTSUGU: Anyway. It was dark. And I was busy making sure everyone was safe. Our group was pretty ragtag, so I was distracted. And I was tired, since we didn't see any yokai.

YURA: *(muttering)* Give me a break.

(Sounds of rattling and ceramics breaking. Rikuo stumbles in, dropping a tea set onto the floor.)

KIYOTSUGU: What are you doing, Rikuo?!

RIKUO: Uh, I'm... I mean... I thought I'd bring some tea.

OIKAWA: Hang in there, Master!

SHIMA: Oikawaaa!

(continued on page 176)

Act 5: The Founding of the Kiyojuji Paranormal Patrol

Act 5:

The Founding of the Kiyojuji Paranormal Patrol

POP
POP
POP
HYUUUUU
...
YOU'RE ...
B
YOU'RE AN ONMYOJI?!
AN...AN EXORCIST!
ISN'T THAT WHAT YOU JUST SAID?!
N
NOD
THEN... THEN...
...THAT THING... JUST NOW...

GRRRAA
WAAAH!!
IT REALLY IS A YOKAI!!
EEEEEEEEEK
YES.
THEY ARE...
...VERY DANGEROUS.
...
IT'S...
IT'S ALL TRUE!!
I WAS RIGHT!!
ONMYOJI... AND YOKAI!
WA HA HA HA HA
I WAS RIGHT!
...

WHO IS THIS GIRL?
I'M NOT SURE, BUT...
...SHE CAN BANISH YOKAI?!
WHISPER
HEY! YUKI-ONNA! WHAT'S AN "ONMYOJI"?
SHAKE SHAKE SHAKE SHAKE
EH?
SHAKE
EHH?!
WE NEED GET OUT OF HERE RIGHT NOW!
MASTER ...
LET'S RUN!
Y... YUKI-ONNA?!
Relax!
YEEE! YEEE!
SHUDDER
I'M AN ONMYOJI. I SPECIALIZE IN EXORCIZING YOKAI.
I'M THE LAST OF MY CLAN.
COME TO THINK OF IT, I'VE HEARD THE NAME "KEIKAIN" ON TV!
Oooh! Him?
THAT WAS MY GRAND-FATHER, HIDEMOTO KEIKAIN.
NO WAY! WHAT IS SOMEONE SO FAMOUS DOING HERE?

THIS PLACE, UKIYOE TOWN, IS WELL KNOWN FOR HIGH SUPERNATURAL ACTIVITY.
REALLY?
RUMOR HAS IT THAT IT'S THE HOME OF THE ACTUAL RULER OF THE YOKAI...
HURK
I'M...
...ON A TRAINING MISSION.
I WANT TO BANISH AS MANY YOKAI AS POSSIBLE!!
THAT WAY...
...I CAN PROVE MY WORTH AS AN ONMYOJI, AND INHERIT MY GRAND-FATHER'S LEGACY!
BEAM
WHAT?! BANISH YOKAI?!
TH- THAT'S...
...INCREDIBLE!! A PRO!! A PRO HAS JOINED...
...MY KIYOJUJI PARA-NORMAL PATROL!

PLEASE!! PLEASE!! WORK WITH US!!
I'M HUNTING A CERTAIN YOKAI!!
CLAP
A CERTAIN YOKAI?
YES!!
HE IS...
...THE MASTER OF NIGHT AND DARKNESS!
I SERIOUSLY NEED TO MEET HIM AGAIN!
DO YOU MEAN...
...THE ONE WHO LEADS THE NIGHT PARADE OF A HUNDRED DEMONS?
TWK
YES.
HE'S THE ONE.
THE LORD OF THE YOKAI!!
B—M
BUT, WHERE DID YOU-
GRIN
CLOP

TOGETHER, WE'LL FIND HIM!
WE WILL FIND THE LORD OF THE YOKAI!!
AH HA HA HA HA HA HA
OOOOM
THIS IS IT! THE FIRST MISSION OF THE KIYOJUJI PARANORMAL PATROL!
GAAH!!!
M-MASTER, WHAT SHOULD WE DO?
WHAT CAN WE DO? NOT MUCH...
POP
POP
POP
POP
GRAAAAH!!
EEEEK!!
DIE!
WHAMM

...
WHEW...
I THOUGHT YOU ALREADY SEALED ITS POWER.
WHAT... DOES THIS MEAN?
YES, IT'S STRANGE.
498 YEN?
THUM THUM
A 50-YEN-OFF COUPON?
THUM THUM THUM
GAH!
I'M SO SORRY! I WAS CARRYING MY SHIKIGAMI IN MY WALLET...
FWIP FWIP
THESE COUPONS AND RECEIPTS MUST HAVE GOTTEN MIXED IN...
It's tough living on my own...
I DON'T UNDER-STAND IT COM-PLETELY, BUT...
...THIS IS REALLY BAD NEWS!!

KATUNK KATUNK
Ukiyoe To
WHAT'S WRONG, KANA?
GLOOM...
YOU DON'T LOOK SO GOOD.
RIKUO...
...WHO WOULD LOOK GOOD AFTER SEEING A MONSTER?
I'm too scared to even go to the bathroom alone.
I SEE. YOU'RE RIGHT.
SHE REALLY HATES BEING SCARED.
ANYWAY, DON'T FORGET ABOUT SUNDAY!
OH... YEAH...
SEE YA!
...
IF SHE HATES SCARY STUFF, WHY'D SHE JOIN A "PARANORMAL PATROL," ANYWAY?
TELL ME, MASTER...
WHY DID YOU MAKE A PROMISE LIKE THAT?

I COULDN'T JUST REFUSE A STRAIGHT-FORWARD REQUEST!
...
IT'S A HUMAN THING.
BESIDES, WE WOULD LOOK SUSPICIOUS OTHER-WISE!
ARE YOU TRYING TO GET ME KILLED?! I'M GOING TO GET SEALED AWAY!!
YOU INVITED...
...THE KIYOJUJI PARANORMAL PATROL INTO THE HEADQUARTERS OF THE NURA CLAN!!
YOUR HOUSE IS BIG AND OLD, NURA.
IT'S PERFECT! OKAY, PEOPLE ...
IT'LL BE FINE! PROBABLY...
WHEN THEY SEE KEIKAIN, EVERYONE WILL BEHAVE THEMSELVES FOR GOOD!!
YOU'RE TAKING THIS WAY TOO LIGHTLY.
YAMMER
HEY, LOOK AT THAT...
A MOTOR-CYCLE GANG. DON'T SEE THAT VERY OFTEN ANYMORE.
YAMMER
IT'S ALL ABOUT KEEPING A LOW PROFILE.
HUH?
VRROOM

THANKS AGAIN, KURATA!!
LATER, BOSS!!
KURATA, YOU'RE THE GREATEST!!
WE'LL COME GET YA TOMORROW TOO!!
FINE.
YEAH.
WAAHOO!! AS LONG AS WE HAVE KURATA, THE HUNDRED DEMONS GANG WILL BE...
...THE MOST FEARED GANG IN TOWN!!

HUH?
SHOCK
AH! MASTER!
SHING
HOW ARE YOU TODAY, SIR?
HAD A LITTLE ERRAND TO RUN WITH THE HUMANS.
I DID MY BEST TO BLEND IN, SO THEY WON'T KNOW I'M YOKAI.
EH?!
MURMUR
MURMUR
YOU'RE STICKING OUT LIKE A SORE THUMB!!!
GEEZ, YOU REALLY DON'T GET IT.
WHAT'S ALL THIS ABOUT?!
WELL... THERE WERE SOME GUYS THAT HAD THEIR EYE ON YOU, SO I WENT TO TEACH THEM A LESSON.
ONE THING LED TO ANOTHER, AND SOMEHOW I ENDED UP BECOMING THEIR LEADER. BUT...WHAT'S A "BROTHERHOOD"?
BR UM MM
WHAT DID YOU DO?
THAT BIKER GUY SCARES ME.
BUT HE'S TREATING THAT KID LIKE HIS BOSS!
PSST
PSST
URK!
ANYWAY, LET'S GO HOME!!
BEFORE WE ATTRACT ANY MORE ATTENTION...
YEAH...
IT'S A LITTLE NOISY HERE...

HUH? SOME-THING'S GOING ON AT THE HOUSE.
EH?
WUH...
WHAT THE ...?!
WA HA HA HA HA

DARRR

WOOOOHOOOO
RAAAH!

IT'S PARTY TIME!!
BWA HA HA HA
DRINK! SING!
WE SEEM TO BE RUNNING LOW ON SAKE.
WHA HA HA
KEE-YAH
IT'S A CELEBRATION OF LORD RIKUO'S TRANSFOR-MATION!
KUBINASHI!! WHY ARE YOU STILL SOBER?!
A HANDSOME YOKAI LIKE YOU IS OUR TICKET WITH THE LADIES!
GLUG GLUG
HEE HEE HEE HEE
I THINK THAT'S THE REASON, ANYWAY!
FWASH

LORD RIKUO! YOU'RE HOME AT LAST!!
EVERYONE!! THE MAN OF THE HOUR HAS ARRIVED!!
COME RIGHT IN!
HEY, SOMEONE BRING MORE SAKE!
SUSHI!
YOU KNOW, YOU HAD US ALL WORRIED FOR A WHILE.
TUP TUP
BUT WE KNEW YOU'D COME TO YOUR SENSES ...
LOOK, NIGHT IS ALMOST UPON US.
SHOW US ALL AGAIN! SHOW US YOUR TRUE FORM!
MASTER!! WHAT ARE YOU DOING?
MY CLASSMATES ARE ALL COMING OVER ON SUNDAY!!
WHAT? NEW RECRUITS?
KRASH
KAKLANK
OF COURSE NOT!!

SHUP
...
SHFF
WA HA HA HA HA
THAT SEEMS TO BE THE REASON FOR THE FESTIVITIES.
AS WE SUSPECTED...
THE HEAD FAMILY CELEBRATES...
...YET DANGER IS NEAR.
FOR IF THE SUPREME COMMANDER'S GRANDSON TRULY HAS AWAKENED...
...WE MUST STRIKE NOW.
WE MUST RID OURSELVES OF HIM ONCE AND FOR ALL.
DM

TRUE STORY!!

– YOKAI DEBATE AT DAWN –

NURA CLAN WHO'S WHO

Setting: *Dawn breaks over the Nura household. Birds chirping.*

KEJORO: What're you doing, lying about like a rag doll?!

KUBINASHI: Oooh, I feel terrible. What a hangover.

KEJORO: You're pathetic! I can't believe you lost against Aotabo and Natto-Kozo! You're the only one who passed out!

NATTO-KOZO: Did someone just say my name?

KEJORO: Yeah. We were just talking about who's got the highest tolerance for sake. Kubinashi here obviously has the lowest.

KUBINASHI: Come now, dear Kejoro....

KEJORO: Don't you try to sweet talk me! I won't fall for that this time.

KUBINASHI: I'm not trying to deceive you. Don't be so stern.

NATTO-KOZO: If you're talking tolerance, isn't Aotabo the guy? He wasn't at the party last night, but his ability to drink is the stuff of legend.

KEJORO: That's what I'm saying.

KUROTABO: Now hold on a minute—

KEJORO: Who said that?!

(Kurotabo emerges from beneath a blanket)

KUROTABO: Ao's the strongest? Give me a break. The last man standing last night was me.

KEJORO: Oh, really?

NATTO-KOZO: I don't know. You were definitely last, but I heard you were eating instead of drinking the whole time.

KUROTABO: Urk!!

KUBINASHI: Well, the sake was certainly disappearing at a fast clip in Kurotabo's vicinity. Maybe the one sitting next to him was actually strongest.

Everyone: ...

KEJORO: That would be me.

KUBINASHI: Ha! You always get the last laugh, Kejoro...

(The End)

Act 6: A Tour of Rikuo's House
UKIYOE TOWN STATION, EAST EXIT.
UKIYOE TOWN
UKIK
A STREET DOWNTOWN.
SKREE
SQUIK SQUIK
AHH!
NO!
AUGH...
NNNGH!
KRAK
HEY! WHAT'S GOING ON OVER THERE?!
TOK
BAH! MORE SEWER RATS...
IT'S PEOPLE LIKE YOU WHO MAKE THIS TOWN—

?!
?!
WUH... WHAT THE...?!
AAAUGH!
SWSH KRAK
SHFF
LIKE ALWAYS...
...
...YOU'RE A RAT WHO DINES ON KITTENS...
... KYŪSO.

Act 6: A Tour of Rikuo's House

BUT, MASTER ...
...WHY DO WE HAVE TO HIDE?!
DANGER! KEEP OUT!! —YUKI-ONNA
EX-TREME COLD!
KEEP OU
TAKING THE DAY OFF! —YUKI-ONNA
THU
YOU'RE ASKING US TO HIDE BECAUSE YOUR HUMAN FRIENDS ARE COMING OVER?!
THUM
LISTEN, THIS IS A YOKAI HOUSE!
WHAT ?!
...
I SEE YOUR POINT...
...BUT PLEASE... THIS IS IN YOUR BEST INTEREST TOO.
WE EXIST TO BE FEARED BY HUMANS!
GRUMBLE
GRUMBLE
JUST WHO DO THESE HUMANS THINK THEY ARE?!
ONE'S THE DESCENDANT OF AN ONMYOJI.
DING DONG

YOKAI QUIZ QUESTION 17!
WHICH OF THE FOLLOWING IS A FIRE YOKAI THAT FLIES ACCOMPANIED BY BIRDS? (A) TSURUBEBI, (B) FURARIBI OR (C) UBAGABI.
UMM... IS IT C?
BZZZZT! THE ANSWER IS B.
YAMMER
YAMMER
KIYOTSUGU'S NOTES
HA HA HA! SHIMA, YOU HAVE A LONG WAY TO GO.
YOU LACK SPIRIT!!
SPIRIT, HUH?
WE'RE GOING TO HAVE KEIKAIN FIRE UP THAT SPIRIT!!
SHE'S A YOKAI PRO!!
HA HA HA HA
SPIRIT, HUH?
ANY-WAY...
...AS PROMISED, THIS MANSION SURE IS RUN-DOWN.
KREEEE
S-SORRY I TOOK SO LONG!
YOU REALLY ARE SLOW, NURA!!
HURRY UP AND GIVE US THE TOUR.

A YOKAI MEETING IN A YOKAI MANSION!!
COME ON, KIYOTSUGU. YOU'RE BEING RUDE TO NURA!
I DON'T CARE!
TH-THEY ALREADY KNOW IT'S A YOKAI MANSION...
W-WE'RE GOING TO BE KILLED...
HIDE! HIDE!
HYUUUUU
KLAK KLAK KLAK
HYUU
...
FEELS LIKE SOME-THING'S LURKING.
SO THIS IS THE KIND OF HOUSE YOU LIVE IN, NURA...
THE ATMOSPHERE IS FANTASTIC. WELL, LET'S BEGIN.
WE'D ALL LIKE TO HEAR...
...KEIKAIN LECTURE US ABOUT YOKAI, SINCE SHE'S A PROFESSIONAL ONMYOJI.
HUH?!

WELL... ALL RIGHT...
FOR STARTERS, THAT DOLL FROM BEFORE... THAT WAS A TYPICAL EXAMPLE ...
...OF A "TSUKUMO-GAMI."
TSU-KUMO-GAMI?
SHIMA!! YOU REALLY DON'T KNOW ANY-THING, DO YOU?!
"AFTER A PERIOD OF ONE HUNDRED YEARS HAVE PASSED, OBJECTS ATTAIN SOULS, TRANSFORM AND PLAY TRICKS ON HUMANS."
TSUKUMO-GAMI ARE YOKAI FORMED FROM THOSE TRANSFORMED, NEGLECTED OBJECTS.
YOKAI CAN BE CATEGORIZED INTO DIFFERENT SPECIES.
SOME HAVE A HUMAN APPEAR-ANCE.
ONI, TENGU, AND KAPPA ARE HUMANOID ENTITIES.
SOME ARE MANIFESTATIONS OF SUPERNATURAL PHENOMENA, LIKE THE FURARIBI MENTIONED EARLIER.
IT'S SAID THAT ONE-THIRD OF YOKAI ARE FIRE YOKAI.
AND THE MAIN OBJECTIVE FOR ALL OF THEM IS FRIGHTENING PEOPLE.
THE MOST PERILOUS ARE THE BEASTS TURNED YOKAI!
MANY OF THEM ARE INTELLIGENT, BUT VERY IRRATIO-NAL.
THEY ARE EX-TREMELY DANGER-OUS!

THEIR ANIMAL DRIVES LEAD THEM TO DECEIVE, CURSE, SLAY AND DEVOUR!!
YOU MUST TAKE CARE NEVER TO COME IN CONTACT WITH THEM!!
ALSO... IT'S SAID THAT THE ONE WHO CONTROLS THE HUNDRED DEMONS...
...IS THE SUPREME COMMANDER OF YOKAI, "NURA-RIHYON."
URK
RUMOR IS...
...HE'S SETTLED DOWN IN *THIS VERY TOWN.*
THUM
THUM
THUM
THUM
EVEN THOUGH NURARI-HYON...
...IS THE MASTER OF YOKAI...
...HE'S SUPPOSED TO BE THE PETTY VILLAIN TYPE...
HE'S THE MAS-TER...
...OF INSPIRING FEAR IN HUMANS. HE'S A "YOKAI'S YOKAI," IF YOU WILL.

BUT...
...IF I CAN DEFEAT HIM, I WILL ATTAIN GREAT HONOR.
SINCE ANCIENT TIMES, WE, THE ONMYOJI, WERE THE ONES WHO WERE CHARGED WITH ERADICATING YOKAI.
IT IS MY DESTINY... AND I WILL SURELY CARRY IT OUT IN THIS TOWN.
SHLP
I BROUGHT TEA.
Yokai Kejoro
SHFF
TINK TINK
SHNIP
PLEASE ENJOY YOUR VISIT.
BOING
WHAT ?! WHO?
TP TP TP
WAS THAT YOUR SISTER ?!
NURA, YOU HAVE DYNAMITE LIKE THAT IN YOUR FAMILY?!

AH...
I REMEMBER HIM SAYING SOMETHING ABOUT A MAID.
A MAID ...?
THUM THUM
SOME-THING ABOUT HER...
THUM THUM
THIS HOUSE... THERE'S SOMETHING... STRANGE ABOUT IT.
THUM THUM
I BEG YOU!! IF YOU ALL SHOW YOUR-SELVES, THEY'LL FIND US OUT!!
I WON'T GO IN AGAIN. THAT GIRL'S DANGER-OUS.
That was a narrow escape.
NOD
NOD
I-I'M SORRY. I WAS IN THE KITCHEN, SO I DIDN'T KNOW...
But... the meal...
EVER SINCE HE GOT INTO MIDDLE SCHOOL, MASTER HAS FALLEN IN WITH A BAD CROWD...
HUMAN SOCIETY IS TRULY FRIGHT-ENING !!
SHUP
SORRY TO KEEP YOU WAITING!

HUH?
SHM
WHERE ARE WE GOING, KEIKAIN?!
TP TP TP TP
WHOA! THEY'RE OUTSIDE!!
TP TP TP
MASTER! YOU PROMISED THIS WOULDN'T HAPPEN!
RUN FOR IT!!
IT CAN'T BE HELPED. IT'S MASTER'S ORDERS.
TCH... ALL BECAUSE OF A MERE HUMAN.
SHE'S SCARY!
I THOUGHT I SENSED A POWERFUL SUPER-NATURAL PRESENCE...
But, I'm not sure.
EH?!
WHAT DO YOU MEAN BY THAT?!

MAYBE THIS HOUSE REALLY IS A YOKAI MANSION!
THEY'RE ALREADY FIGURING IT OUT!
OH, NO!
THERE GOES MY PEACEFUL LIFE...
HEY EVERYONE, LET'S GO BACK INSIDE AND TALK ABOUT YOKAI!
AH!! WHY DON'T WE PLAY A GAME INSTEAD ?!
HOW ABOUT A GAME TO SEE WHO CAN NAME THE MOST YOKAI?
NOT A CHANCE.
NURA, YOU'RE GOING TO EXPLAIN ALL THIS IN DETAIL LATER.
RMB
B-BBMP
B-BBMP
BATHING HALL?
BATHING HALL
WATER ...
I KNOW I'M BEING RUDE, NURA, BUT I HAVE TO TAKE A LOOK INSIDE.
EH ?!
SHOOOOM

Nura Family Grand Bathing Hall
...
PLING
SEE? NO ONE'S HERE.
PLIP
PLIP
...
NO ONE? HMM.
FWAM
I SMELL SOMETHING SUSPICIOUS IN HERE!
Altar Room
WHOA... AMAZING.
BUDDHA STATUES IN ALL THEIR GILDED SPLENDOR...
Nuri-Botoke: A yokai statue that pops out its eyes.
GAH! IT'S NURI-BOTOKE.
KEEP THOSE EYES IN THEIR SOCKETS!!
HM?
THIS STATUE...
GASP

DOOOOM
Cross-section
HMM ...
?
A-AMAZING, AREN'T THEY? HA HA HA
SUCH BAD TASTE... THEY'RE MY GRANDPA'S.
GRANDPA WILL GET MAD IF WE TOUCH THEM.
PUSH PUSH
SEE? THERE'S NO ONE HERE. LET'S GO BACK.
I... I GUESS ...
I THINK I'D BETTER PUT A CHARM ON IT FOR THE MOMENT, THOUGH...
TK
YEEEK!
MASTER, PLEASE TAKE IT OFF!
L-LATER !!
HOW DISAP-POINTING, THERE WAS NOTHING THERE.
TMP TMP
SHIVER SHAKE
Y-YES, IT'S STRANGE ...
...
SO, THERE WAS NOTHING OUT OF THE ORDINARY, AFTER ALL.
TIP TIP
CLOSE CALL!
I'M GLAD THE CLAN COULD SENSE THE DANGER.
WHEW ...

SHOOOM
OH, RIKUO.
THESE YOUR FRIENDS?
...!!
AH.
THANK YOU FOR YOUR HOSPI-TALITY.
HER "BIG GAME" JUST SHOWED UP!!!
OOOH... YOU SO RARELY HAVE FRIENDS OVER.
CARE FOR SOME CANDY?
EVERY-ONE...
...PLEASE LOOK AFTER MY GRANDSON.
BEAM
AH... YES...
YOU CAN ENTRUST HIM TO US, SIR!!
BUT, THIS CANDY TASTES TER-RIBLE!
NO ONE IS NOTICING THAT HE'S...
Nurarihyon can pass unnoticed even when entering someone's home without permission—such is the nature of this yokai...
The yokai you're after is right in front of you.

HONESTLY, YOU SHOULD TAKE A LESSON FROM ME.
ALL THIS DRAMA OVER ONE LITTLE ONMYOJI GIRL!
WHY, IN MY YOUTH, I USED TO WALK INTO THE MAIN ONMYOJI HEADQUARTERS AND HELP MYSELF TO THEIR FOOD.
ONLY THE SUPREME COMMANDER COULD ACCOMPLISH SUCH A FEAT...
UGH
THAT SAID, AT THE VERY LEAST YOU ALL SHOULD BE ABLE TO CONCEAL YOUR SUPERNATURAL PRESENCE.
OKAY, BUT WHAT ABOUT US?
CHANGE INTO HUMAN FORM.
MURMUR
MURMUR
WHAT ABOUT THOSE WITH SEVERED HEADS?
ATTACH THEM!
YAK YAK
THERE ARE MANY DIFFERENT APPROACHES TO IT, SUCH AS REVERTING BACK INTO AN OBJECT IF YOU ARE A TSUKUMO-GAMI.
YAMMER
OOOH... I'M SO TIRED...
YAMMER
FIP
FIP

HEH HEH...
HELLO, SCHOOL-GIRL...
WHERE ARE YOU GOING?
...
HA HA HA
YURA!
AH! UM, IENAGA?
THIS AREA GETS A LITTLE DICEY AROUND THIS TIME OF NIGHT.
EH?
LET'S GO.
WHERE DOES YOUR FAMILY LIVE?
YAK YAK
OH, I LIVE BY MY-SELF.
...
I... CLEARLY NEED TO TRAIN MORE.
I REALLY THOUGHT THERE WAS SOMETHING THERE.
I WAS SO RUDE TO NURA.

WOW!
YOU GIRLS REALLY SEEM DOWN. HOW TERRIBLE...
FINDERS, KEEPERS! I THINK I SHOULD TAKE YOU BOTH OVER TO MY CLUB.
OR, WOULD YOU RATHER GO SOMEWHERE ELSE? NOTHING WRONG WITH THAT !!
EH ?
WSH
SNIK SNIK
COME ON, HANG OUT WITH ME!
...
LET'S GO, YURA.
SWIP
EH? WAIT...
KRCH! KRCH!
WHAT IN THE ...?
STAY BACK, IENAGA.
YURA ?

SNIK
SNIK
OH, DON'T BE SO COLD, LITTLE KITTENS. ♡
THUM
THUM
THUM
YOU TWO... KNOW THE THIRD.
SH
THE NIGHT IS YOUNG!
FF FF
COME, LET ME GNAW ON YOU...UNTIL THERE'S NOTHING LEFT BUT BONES... ♡
Beast-Yokai Kyuso

TRUE STORY!!

A MEETING OF THE KIYOJUJI PARANORMAL PATROL

– KEIKAIN'S FRUSTRATION –

(continued from page 136)

TSURARA: So what am I supposed to call you? Oh yeah. No honorifics, right. Right, Ri...Rikuo. R-Rikuo...

RIKUO: Just call me Nura, like the other kids.

TSURARA: Oh! Th-that's right... but Lord Rikuo, you can just call me Tsurara....

SHIMA: What are you two whispering about?

KIYOTSUGU: Hey, can we please get back to the matter at hand? Yokai, people!

YURA: *(under her breath)* Finally. They really made me wait.

MAKI: Hi, guys, thanks for waiting! You would not believe how long it takes Torii to pick out a drink.

TORII: What?! Look who's talking! Don't blame me!

MAKI: Hee hee! Okay, so I'm busted.

YURA: *(under her breath)* Who cares?!

KIYOTSUGU: Okay then, since we're all here...

YURA: *(to herself)* Don't do roll call! Just get on with it!!

KIYOTSUGU: Anyway. About the abandoned school building...

KANA: I am so sorry for being late!

YURA: **Just get on with it!!**

(The End)

Setting: *Rikuo is cleaning up the tea he spilled on the floor.*

KIYOTSUGU: You really are something else, Rikuo.

TSURARA: Are you okay, Master?

RIKUO: *(whispers)* Yuki-Onna, I told you not to call me "master" at school!

TSURARA: I'm sorry, Lord Rikuo!

RIKUO: "Lord Rikuo" is just as bad!

HFF
HIS...
HIS FACE!
HE'S A MONSTER!!
THE LONG NIGHT BEGINS!
Act 7: Rikuo Goes to First Street

Act 7: Rikuo Goes to First Street

FWOOOOO
SKTCH
SKTCH
SKTCH
WAAH!
NO!
DOOM
WHAT ARE THEY?
YURA?
...
THEY'RE YOKAI.
JUST LIKE I EXPLAINED THIS AFTERNOON...
...THEY'RE BEAST-YOKAI.
...
EH?!
THEY CAN'T BE REASONED WITH.
THEY'RE DANGEROUS!

COME QUIETLY, AND WE PROMISE WE'LL MAKE IT PAINLESS.
HEH HEH HEH
YOU SURE SOUND CONFIDENT...
...FOR A PACK OF RODENTS.
GRIN
WHAT?
SHFF...
STAY BEHIND ME, IENAGA.
EH?!
SHFF
ALL RIGHT, BOYS...
...DO IT.
WAH!

TMP
UHO-TENHO...
TMP
HUH?
TMP
TENNAI...
TENSHO...
TMP
TENHO-TENNIN!
SKRIT
?!
KEN-KON-GENKO-RITEI!
FLIP
TAKE FORM, MY SHIKIGAMI!
FLIP
BAH
TAN...
...RO!
WOSH

WHOA!
HOLY ...
WHAT THE—?!
A WOLF ?!
WUH ...
VWOOSH
GAH!
KRAK

AUGH!
WHOK
GRRRRRR
WAAH!
BAM
HURK
GRRR
TANRO...
CRRRRR
YAAH!!
THOSE RATS...
...DEVOUR THEM.
CRAP!
H
WS

GYAAAAH!!
YEEEEK!!
WHAT IS THAT THING?!
GYAAA
TSU-BASA!!
AAH
SU-GURU!!
S-SHE'S...
YEEE
...USING A SHIKIGAMI!
SHE'S A MAGICIAN!
AN ON-MYOJI!!
AND NO ORDINARY ONE, EITHER!!

FOOOOOM
GOOD BOY, TANRO.
HRRR
B-BOSS?
SHUT UP.
KYUSO, WHO IS THAT CHICK?!
KYUSO, HUH?
SO, YOU'RE RAT YOKAI WITH A TASTE FOR KITTENS...
...THE HUMAN KIND.
AND YOU HUNT THEM OUT IN THE OPEN, LIKE THIS?
HA HA HA...
MAN...
THE THIRD SURE CAN PICK HIS FRIENDS.
FWIP
TOK
TOK
SLIDE
YOU REALLY SHOULD AVOID VIOLENT TYPES LIKE HIM.
WAP
PAWS OFF, RAT!!

HUH?
...
SHFF
SWIP
SWIP
...?
UH-OH.
WHISPER
BAD MOVE. SHOW'S OVER FOR HER.
WHISPER

SKITCH
AUGH!!
SKITCH
RATS! NOOO!!
SKITCH
SPIN
STOP!!
SHE DIDN'T DO ANY-THING TO YOU!!
?!
TAN-RO!
GIVE IT UP. I CAN BRING FORTH AS MANY RATS AS I NEED.
!
?
NOW, BEHAVE YOURSELF AND DISMISS YOUR SHIKIGAMI.
NO! STOP!
SKITCH
SKITCH
G-GET OUT!
SKITCH
AND DON'T EVEN THINK OF TRYING A DIFFER-ENT SHIKIGAMI.
...
PAFF

WHY ...
WHY ARE YOU... DOING THIS... TO US?
YURA ?!
NOW, HANDLE THEM DELICATELY, BOYS.
THAT'S SOME VALUABLE BAIT.

HYUUUU
THERE. FINALLY DONE.
WHAT A PAIN, REBUILDING ZEN'S HOUSE.
YAK YAK
BEAMMM
AO! KURO! WELCOME HOME!!
DINNER'S ALL READY!
IT'S NOT MY HOME COOKING TODAY, THOUGH!
WHAT?
SHE SURE IS CHEERY.
HE HE
YOU'RE SO TRANS-PARENT, YUKI-ONNA.
THE MINUTE KEIKAIN LEFT, YOU PERKED RIGHT UP.
OKAY! LET'S HAVE ROLL CALL!
I WANNA MAKE SURE EVERY-ONE'S OKAY!
I WONDER IF SHE REALIZES THAT SHE'LL BE SEEING HER AGAIN AT SCHOOL TOMORROW.

DOK DOK
MAS-TER!
LORD RIKUO!
HUH?
A RAT?
BOW
A PLEASURE TO MEET YOU.
I AM A REPRE-SENTATIVE OF THE KYUSO CLAN.
THE KYUSO CLAN?
YACK YACK
WHO ARE THEY?
YES.
WE LIVE IN ON FIRST STREET IN UKIYOE TOWN.
I CAME HERE... BECAUSE I SAW SOME-THING.
YOUR FRIENDS, YURA KEIKAIN AND KANA IENAGA, WERE...
HOSTS? WHAT DO YOU MEAN? KIDNAPPED?
WHAT'S GOING ON?!
WHY THEM?!

YAK YAK
HUH? WHERE'D MASTER GO?
FWIP FWIP
OH, NOW THAT YOU MENTION IT...
...
"BUT LORD RIKUO... SHE IS AN ONMYOJI."
"I DON'T THINK IT'S WISE TO INVOLVE THE FAMILY."
DID SOMETHING HAPPEN AS THEY WERE WALKING HOME?
"DON'T WORRY, MY CLANSMEN WILL BE THERE TO HELP, SO YOU CAN GO IT ALONE."
THIS IS THE PLACE!
Club Chu
IT'S A NIGHT-CLUB ...
WHAT'S GOING ON?!
DOOM
THUNK
NNGH ...
...
WHERE AM I?

HELLO, THERE. AWAKE NOW?
MR. SO-CALLED "THE THIRD"?
M
...
WHO ARE YOU?!
THE THIRD?
WAIT! YOU'RE A YOKAI?
ARE YOU IN THE NURA CLAN?

OW ...!
SHOW PROPER RESPECT WHEN YOU ADDRESS LORD KYUSO!
NO-BODY HERE AN-SWERS TO YOU, MORON!
DM
LORD KYUSO IS...
...THE EMPER-OR OF THE NIGHT!
THE EMPEROR ...?
LISTEN UP, PEEWEE.
THE YOKAI WORLD HAS EXPANDED ITS VARIETY SINCE THE OLD DAYS. THERE ARE STRONGER, MORE EVIL SYNDICATES NOW.
AND WE'RE GOING TO TAKE THAT EVILDOING TO A WHOLE NEW LEVEL.
...
THAT'S WHY...
...WE CAN'T ALLOW SOME HALF-HEARTED WIMP LIKE YOU TO TAKE OVER.
!!
AH!

KANA?! KEIKAIN ?!
IT'S FOR THE THE GOOD OF THE SYNDICATE.
THERE'S NO MORE ROOM FOR THOSE OLD SCHOOL YOKAI IN OUR BRAVE NEW WORLD.
SO, WE'RE GOING TO RUN THE NURA CLAN.
WE WANT YOU TO STEP DOWN AND DECLARE THAT YOU WON'T TAKE UP THE TITLE OF THE THIRD.
GOT IT?!
THE THIRD?! I DON'T CARE ABOUT THAT!!
LET THEM GO!! BOTH OF THEM !!
UGH ...
SNAP
IT KILLS ME TO THINK THAT YOU'RE SET TO BE THE LEADER OF THE YOKAI WORLD!
WAM
WAM
HOW DARE YOU SAY THAT SO EASILY, HALF-BREED?!

The End of Volume 1:
Becoming the Lord of Pandemonium

True Tales of the Nura Clan

Extra

Family Feud

SO, WE'RE HAVING TRYOUTS! TRANSFORMATION TRYOUTS!!
WHOA!!
A PAIR?!
WHY THE HOT WATER?
OOOH! I NOMINATE ME!
NOBODY CAN PASS FOR HUMAN LIKE I CAN!!
YEAH!! DO IT!!
TAKE IT OFF!
SHFF
FAP
FWUMP
OOOH
HOW'S THIS? I'M A DOCTOR!
BLING
BLING
WOULDN'T THIS BE PERFECT FOR THE SCHOOL INFIRMARY?!
CLAP CLAP CLAP CLAP
WHOOP!
YES!! WELL DONE, KEJORO!!
WE HAVE A FEMALE!
A SEXY LADY DOCTOR! THE MASTER WILL BE HAPPY TOO!
YAK YAK
I CHANGED TOO!

WUH-HO!
A BACKPACK! KAWAI—
WHAT DO YOU THINK?
IT'S...
IT'S...
10.0
10.0
10.0
YEAH, IT'S BETTER TO POSE AS A CLASSMATE!
BECAUSE KIDS ALMOST NEVER GO SEE THE NURSE!
Y-YOUUU...
YAK YAK
RRRRRRRG
WE GOTTA COME UP WITH A NAME! FUTAGAWA? IKAWA?
GLARE
YOU LOLICON JERKS!!
RIOT!
YOU STUPID YOKAI DON'T APPRECIATE THE CHARMS OF A GROWN WOMAN!!
GET OVER HERE!! I'LL ROLL YOU UP LIKE MAKI!!
GRAAAH!
OI! YUKI-ONNA! HELP US! AHH!
?

KUBINASHI'S PERFECT FOR THE BOY'S ROLE!
ALL HE NEEDS IS A SCARF!
NO, LET ME TRY! KAPPA MAKE BETTER KIDS!
WAIT, WAIT!!
FMP
SHFF
AOTABO ?!
OCCUPIED
EVERY-ONE KNOWS I'M CLOSEST TO MASTER.
WE'VE BEEN TO-GETHER EVER SINCE HE WAS A BABY.
OKAY, I GET IT...
YEAH, YOU'D MAKE A GOOD P.E. TEACH—
YOU WANT TO BE A SCHOOL-BOY ?!
DOOM
THAT'S IMPOSSIBLE!
DOOM
BA
IS THERE A PROB-LEM ?!
BM
He went on to terrorize the human world in another way.
That's how he became the leader of the Hundred Demons motorcycle gang.
THE END
Extra
True Tales of the Nura Clan: Family Feud

IN THE NEXT VOLUME...

RIKUO VS. GYUKI

When the Kyuso yokai clan kidnaps Rikuo's classmates Kana and Yura, Rikuo transforms into his yokai form to save them. But the plot is far from over. It turns out that Gyuki, a top officer in the Nura clan, secretly masterminded the attack! Unfortunately, Rikuo learns of this deceit just as he's embarking on a camping trip to a mountain renowned for yokai activity. Is Rikuo walking into a trap?!

AVAILABLE APRIL 2011!